THE GAME

·

ENJOYING GOLF
ON & OFF THE COURSE

BERNIE NAJAR

WITH MATTHEW RUDY

FOREWORD BY THOMAS L. FRIEDMAN

Printed in the United States of America

First Printing, 2017

ISBN-13: 978-1981634781
ISBN-10: 1981634789

Bernie Najar
Director of Instruction
Caves Valley Golf Club
2910 Blendon Rd
Owings Mills, MD 21117
www.bernienajar.com

Designed by Tim Oliver (timothypoliver.com)

"The Game" is dedicated to my beautiful, smart and devoted wife, Susan Najar. You have taught me not to wait for everything to be perfect before you decide to enjoy the journey of life. You are my motivation. To my fantastic Mother, siblings, family, friends, and mentors thank you for your love and encouragement.

CONTENTS

FOREWORD | Tom Friedman

Gary Player was fond of remarking that "the more I practice, the luckier I get." There is a lot to that quote. My only tweak would be: the more lessons I take the luckier I get.

I've been taking lessons since I was 7 or 8 years old at the club I grew up at outside of Minneapolis—and I am now 64! I actually love taking lessons. I always arrive with anticipation: where will the hidden secret be found this time? The golf swing is such a simple quick motion and yet so many different teachers have managed to look at that motion of mine from different angles and tell me something I didn't know—takeaway, speed, attack angle, head angle, finish, turn, tempo—something that helped me for a day or a week or forever.

All of this is to say, I am a connoisseur of teaching professionals. And none has taught me more about all aspects of the game—mind and body, putting and chipping, hozzle and hitches, soil, soul and sole—than Bernie Najar. And so it is a treat for me to write this introduction to his first golf book.

Although my day job is writing the foreign affairs column for the New York Times—more Persian Gulf than fairway golf—thinking about golf and playing as often as I can is my all-consuming hobby. And besides playing, the thing I enjoy doing most is taking playing lessons with Bernie. You can demonstrate a lot to a teacher about what is right and wrong with your swing or posture or alignment when you stand on the practice range and hit balls. But while range lessons demonstrate, playing lessons reveal.

That's where the teacher can see not just your swing, but your pace between shots; not just your smile on the good ones, but your attitude after the bad ones; not just your weight shift, but how you line up to a real target; not just your pressure-free motion, but how you swing under pressure on the course when the flare goes up and teacher is watching.

To put it another way, the best teachers always answer both the question you came with—how do I cure my slice?—as well as questions you didn't come with but your actions on the course reveal that you should have been asking. It's been through our many playing lessons over the past couple of years that I have had a chance to listen to Bernie talk out this book—making for a delightful afternoon of swing thoughts and book thoughts. My kind of day! Not every student can afford a playing lesson, so this book is the next best thing. Take it out on the course and think of it as your own playing lesson with Bernie.

The best golf teachers understand four things: physics, geometry, geography and psychology. Bernie addresses all four in this book, as he does in his lessons. The golf swing always starts with a geography quiz: How far away is that target and how is it set in the landscape? Elevated? On a ledge? In a bowl? Then comes the geometry lesson. At what angle and speed do I have to launch this little white ball to match, or take advantage of, the geography and get as close as possible to the hole, taking into account wind and heat as well. Then comes the physics: How do I move my body arms, legs and weight—and at what speed—to ensure that the ball solves this geography-geometry equation, or comes as close as possible to do doing so. And, finally, what emotional and psychological mindset do I need to increase the odds that my body and arms will move into the ideal launch positions—so I will score as best I can and derive the most enjoyment?

That's the core of this book. It's all about how to increase your ability to assess the geography, plot the geometry, then generate the right psychology to increase the odds of getting your personal physics to launch the ball close or into the hole—and do it in a way that increases the fun for you and your partners, no matter what everyone's skill level. In plain English, it's about how to hit a vast array of golf shots and manage a vast array of situations on the golf course so you and your partners can create a vast array of memories.

Some teachers are good demonstrators. They teach by saying "stand over there and watch this..." Some are great communicators—they come up with different ways of saying the same thing about ball position or alignment or swing speed—until they hit on just the right message that penetrates *your* brain. Some are great psychologists who are deft at finding the calming pre-swing thought or pre-shot routine that promotes the right physics. Bernie has been *Golf Digest's* number-one rated teacher in Maryland and a *Golf Magazine* Top 100 teacher because he is good at all three. In golf instruction terms he has an "all-around game."

The commentator Paul Harvey was quoted as saying once that "golf is a game in which you yell fore, shoot six and write down five." Not for me, and I suspect not for a lot of golfers. Golf for me is an eternal quest to improve at something I love, and derive the satisfaction from seeing the input of practice and lessons produce a better output on the course under pressure. Getting better just by giving myself putts or putting down the score I felt I deserved would take away all the fun for me, because a round of golf is not just a total score. It's a journey.

Each and every round is a journey of discovery about yourself and how you respond to good and bad breaks. It's a journey of discovery about your playing partners. It's a journey of discovery about some new, and often exotic, terrain, or new parts and angles of a very familiar terrain. And, if you love the game as I do, it's an everlasting journey in search of self-improvement—always trying to get my geography, geometry, physics and psychology in perfect alignment.

There is no better navigator for this journey than Bernie Najar and no better map than this book.

THOMAS L. FRIEDMAN
New York Times Foreign Affairs Columnist
and Staff Writer for Golf Digest

INTRODUCTION | How to Use This Book

TAKE A LOOK AROUND my teaching studio at Caves Valley and it's easy to see that the information available to a player today is way, way different than it was even 10 years ago.

With force plates, radar systems and 3D cameras, you can measure almost anything you want to know about the swing. Fitting carts have hundreds of different head and shaft combinations, so you can have literally almost anything you want in your hand when you swing. Wedges and putters can now be customized to the tiniest degree to fit your course conditions, your eye and your stroke. And with a crank of a wrench, you can completely change the playing characteristics of your driver (or even your hybrid) before you go and play.

It's a great time to be a player.

But.

As anybody who has ever searched for an instruction video on YouTube knows, having access to an unlimited amount of information doesn't mean you'll find the *right* information.

And even if you find the right information, if you aren't sure how to use it, it won't do you much good. Identifying the problem is only the first part of the process. You have to know what to do next.

That's where *The Game* comes in.

My job as a teacher is to organize and prioritize information for my students. As a coach, my job is to reinforce these concepts and to motivate my players to enjoy the game and achieve their goals. In *The Game*, my goal is to help you with some of that same filtering. We're going to talk about eight of the most common questions and situations players have in the game, and I'm going to share my favorite answers to those questions.

Want to know how to hit better tee shots? We'll cover that. Or how to be a better partner in a team event? I'm sure you want to know how to get up and down more often.

What makes this book different?

You can find plenty of information about the basic mechanics of the golf swing, and advice about hitting different kinds of shots. We're going to talk about some of that, but in this book, I'm going to give you 360-degree solutions for each of those questions.

What does getting off the tee better mean? You have to know how to set up and swing your driver, but you also need to know how to get the right clubs in your hand, and the right strategy to pick for different kinds of holes. When does it make sense to hit driver, and when should you play a different club? And how do you pull it together and hit a shot when you really need one—especially after you hit the last one in the junk?

We'll cover it all.

We're also going to go beyond the standard how-to swing subjects and cover the "soft skills" every player needs to play his or her best golf.

How do you get the most out of your next golf lesson? How do you get better at competition—no matter what your level? There's an art and strategy to both of those things. If you love golf, you probably watch a lot of it on television, and read about it in magazines and online. You might as well get the most out of those experiences, and learn how to absorb the best bits of information into your own game and filter out the rest. I'll show you how.

You can turn the page and start from the beginning, but *The Game* is designed to be a reference book. You can pick the question or problem you want to solve today and go straight to it. It's also designed to be a step-by-step reminder for when you need to come back for a refresher course. Even the best players go through a tune-up phase at the beginning of a season, after they've put the clubs away for a few weeks.

My goal for you is the same as it is for every student who comes and sees me. I want you to swing the club better, but more importantly, I want you to enjoy the entire golf experience. To do that, we're going to focus on improving your overall golf skills—both on and off the course—so that you're building great relationships with the people around you in the game.

And that's when golf is really at its best.

ABOUT ME

SINCE 2012, I've been the Director of Instruction at Caves Valley Golf Club in Owings Mills, MD—one of the premier clubs in the country. At Caves Valley, the top goal is to provide our members and guests with a world-class golf experience that encompasses everything from how they swing the club to how they enjoy the camaraderie of their friends out on the patio.

Back when I was working on my finance degree at the American University, in Washington D.C., my Business Policy and Strategy professor, Dr. Richard Linowes, asked everyone in the class to write a mission statement on what we wanted to accomplish in our careers over the next ten years, and how we planned to achieve it.

For me, this was a powerful exercise, and in my statement, I wrote about wanting to help golfers improve through a comprehensive teaching program. You can probably guess that Dr. Linowes was surprised to find that one of his finance students was planning to be a golf pro—and he gave me some candid feedback about my career choice and objectives. He chuckled and made me promise to check in with him in ten years to let him know how I was doing.

That exercise—and that feedback—was a huge motivator for me to continue to do everything I can to improve my skills and knowledge so I can continue to help players improve their games. That has meant a continuous effort to learn not just how the club should move, but also about fitness, clubfitting and the psychology and process of learning.

In the years since I attended to Dr. Linowes' class, I've accumulated a wealth of information. It has certainly helped me improve as a teacher but it has also shown me just how much conflicting information is out there potentially confusing even the most dedicated learner.

I'm committed to helping people sort through that information, and I feel incredibly blessed to have met and worked with some of the brightest minds in the game—people who have shaped both me and my teaching.

I'm incredibly fortunate to be part of the Caves Valley team, at one of the best teaching facilities in the world. My friend Dennis Satyshur, Caves Valley's Director of Golf, is the ultimate team leader and who makes my job so special. Dennis is an unbelievable mentor, and his team approach provides our members and guests with a world class experience each time they come to Caves. To be a part of the team at Caves Valley, is a dream come true thanks to our Chairman, Steve Fader. Mr. Fader's vision and dedication to the future success of Caves Valley Golf Club builds on the leadership of Les Disharoon and Tony Deering.

I'm also grateful to the members at Caves Valley and Woodholme Country Club for their friendship, support and encouragement over the years. You couldn't find a finer group of people to spend time with on and off the lesson tee.

Here's to enjoying golf, on and off the course!

BERNIE NAJAR
Owings Mills, MD
December 1, 2017

CHAPTER 1

How to Figure Out What Shots

Are Killing Your Score

"Knowing yourself is the beginning of all wisdom" — *Aristotle*

HANDICAPS ARE A NICE, clean way of comparing your score to somebody else's, and for getting a general overview of your game.

But handicaps don't tell you where you're losing the shots that are the difference between you and even par.

And even though there's probably nobody more familiar with your game than you, figuring out where those lost shots are happening isn't as obvious as you think.

When a new student comes to me for a lesson, we start with the same conversation. I want to know what your scoring range is, and what your goals are. I want you to tell me about your game. Some players come in with the general idea that they want to get better. Others come in with very specific issues they want to address—they can't get off the tee. They can't get out of a bunker. They have a terrible slice.

They're looking to me to give them some direction about where to put their time and effort.

If you come in and tell me you want to reduce your handicap from 15 to 10, that's fine, but it's also incomplete. What kind of player are you?

Are you somebody who plays a lot of rounds, but doesn't practice much?

Are you a competitive handicap player who is a regular lesson taker?

Are you somebody who tinkers on the practice range but doesn't play much?

Within each of those categories, you could have a handicap number that looks similar to the player in the next bay at the practice area, but you could have totally different games—both in how you make your scores and the way you approach improvement.

Let me use two of my students as examples. They both have indexes between 11 and 12, but that's pretty much where the similarities end.

The first student is in his 40s. He's a busy guy, with lots of work responsibilities. His index was as low as 5 when he was just out of college, but he doesn't have as much time to play now. He's a powerful player off the tee, but doesn't have as much polish on his short game. He loses shots around the green and with his putter.

The second student is in his late 50s. He was late to the game, starting about ten years ago. He's consistently improved over the years, but his main limitation is that he doesn't feel like he hits it far enough off the tee. That's a problem at his home course, where a couple of the par-4s are borderline too long for him to reach in regulation even from the white tees. He retired early, so he has plenty of time to both practice and play.

If you matched those two up in a club tournament, the handicap numbers would say they could give each other a good match. But a lot would depend on the way the course was set up—and how much the first player had been playing lately.

It's obvious those two players have different games. And on the surface, it might seem obvious which shots are hurting them the most. But the only way to be sure is to get a snapshot of your entire game.

The best way to do that is to pick a six-hole stretch at your home course that has a nice variety of challenges. There's a par-3, a par-5, a hard par-4 and a hole that you feel like you could make a good score on.

Using a "scorecard" like the one here, you're going to ask yourself a series of questions about your game. The answers will give you insight on what you need to work on, and where to start.

OFF THE TEE

- Did you hit the Fairway?
- Did you have a reasonable shot to the green in regulation Y/N
- If you missed the fairway, did you miss left or right?
- Did you incur any penalty shot(s)?

APPROACH SHOTS

- Did you hit the green in regulation and what club did you use? Y/N and Club Used?
- If yes, how far was your 1st putt from the hole?
- If you missed the green, did you miss left or right?
- If you missed the green, did you miss long or short?

CATEGORY 1 SHORT GAME SHOTS (INSIDE 30 YARDS)

- What type of shot did you play? (Bunker shot, Pitching, Chipping, etc...)
- Did you hit the green? Y/N
- If you didn't hole your shot, did it end up long or short?
- How far was your first putt from the hole?

CATEGORY 2 WEDGE PLAY (OUTSIDE 30 YARDS)

- What Wedge Did You Use?
(Pitching Wedge, Gap Wedge, Sand Wedge, Lob Wedge)
- Did you hit the green? Y/N
- If your shot didn't go in, did it end up long or short?
- How far was your first putt from the hole?

PUTTING

- How far was your first putt from the hole?
- Did you 1-Putt? Y/N
- If you didn't 1-Putt, how far was your 2nd putt from the hole?
- On your missed putts, where you long or short, on the low side,
or on the high side?
- Green reading

TRACK AT LEAST 6-HOLES WHEN YOU PLAY (2 PAR 3S, 2 PAR 4S, 2 PAR 5S TO GET A SNAP SHOT OF YOUR GAME. TRACK ALL 18 FOR MORE INFORMATION.

Additional resources that I recommend for tracking your game are available at:
Pete Sanders — ShotByShot.com • Scott Fawcett — PlayingLesson.com •
Mark Brodie's book *Every Shot Counts*

After six holes, you're going to have a pretty good snapshot of what you do in your game. If you're missing tee shots in a consistent direction, you'll know. If you have weaknesses in your short game, they'll be revealed. When I ask my players to do this, they usually pick up on an issue they already know they had—but they almost always find a problem spot they didn't know they had or a shot they thought they hit well but they really didn't.

For example, some players dread bunker shots, and will do anything to stay out of them. That fear hurts their accuracy on approach shots, because they're actually picking clubs and aiming points away from the appropriate target. So when they evaluate their approach game, they feel like it's a weakness when really it's the bunker shots that are causing the problems.

The same chain reaction of struggles happens with tee shots. Maybe you feel like you're decent off the tee, but you really struggle with long irons and hybrids. But the reality might be that you're missing a lot of fairways with your driver and putting pressure on your long game by having to play a lot of hybrids from the rough. You might need work on both of those issues, but it's great to know which one is the most pressing.

Once you have an overall map of your score and where you lose shots, you can make a plan to improve those shots.

How much do you need to improve?

That depends on what scores you want to shoot.

If you want to be a bogey golfer—which, by the way, is better than most players in the game—there is a very specific profile you need to achieve. You need four primary skills.

▷ You need to drive the ball in play far enough to get near the green in two shots.

▷ You need the ability to consistently hit a ball 160 yards (130 for women) near the green on an approach shot.

▷ You need short game skills that will allow you to consistently get on the green in a position where you have a chance to one-putt, you'll definitely two-putt and you'll rarely three-putt.

▷ You need a basic game plan to manage your game and pick the right shots at the right times.

When you think about your overall handicap profile and game, and add in the information you get from charting your skills, it'll be pretty obvious which part of the game needs to be your starting point. And that's just as true if you're trying to be a bogey golfer as it is if your goal is to be a scholarship college player. Only the bar you use to measure yourself is different.

How so?

If I'm working with a good high school player who wants to play college golf, we examine similar things, but with more detail.

▷ Can you control your shots for both distance and trajectory?

▷ Can you move the ball both ways on demand?

▷ Can you consistently hit approach shots within 30 feet of the hole?

▷ Can you hit driver long enough to have middle and short irons into most par 4's?

▷ Is your miss pattern predictable?

▷ Are you able to confidently pick targets off the tee?

▷ Are you able to play par 5s consistently under par?

▷ Is your average short game shot inside five feet from the hole?

The last checkpoint—leaving short game shots five feet or less—is extremely important, and for reasons you probably guess.

PGA Tour players are the best in the world, and they make a lot of putts. From three feet, they make 99 percent of their putts. Move out to five feet, and the number is still 90 percent. From six feet, it drops to 69 percent. At eight feet, a tour player makes 50 percent.

Those players play on the best conditioned greens, and they're the best at what they do. For the rest of us, five or six feet is a good distance to feel like you have a better than average chance to make the putt.

If your short game is mediocre, and you're leaving yourself a lot of 10-footers, you're going to make a lot of bogeys because you can't get up and down. That's true even if you're the best putter on the planet.

Each foot you move farther from the hole, the odds get worse. So the better your short game gets, the better your putting stats are going to look. You're going to make fewer bogeys from failing to get up and down, and you're going to make more birdies.

Improve both skills—short game and putting—and you're going to get two bites at the same apple.

Physical skill improvement is at the heart of lowering your handicap, but the mental component is extremely important as well. It's just as much of a skill as knowing how to hit a variety of shots.

I'll give you two examples.

First, players at every level are hard on themselves about bad results in a way that is disproportionate to their skill level. If you're an 18-handicapper and you hit a 200-yard flare off the tee that stays in the fairway and on the right side to approach the green, the natural tendency is to kick yourself for the weak drive. But relatively speaking, that result isn't bad. It could have been better, but you're still in position to play the hole.

Or, you might have an uphill 10-footer for par that you really want to make. When it doesn't go in, you beat yourself up. But the odds say you're going to make that putt far less than 50 percent of the time.

The turbulence you cause yourself with those negative thoughts hurts your confidence not only on the next shot you're going to play but also the next time you find yourself in the same situation. By having a realistic feel for what "good," "average" and "bad" results are, you're keeping your game in perspective and your emotional equilibrium in check.

And once you actually improve those skills, you're giving yourself a powerful boost to those mental skills as well. As we were saying before, if you hate bunker shots and you have a hard shot that needs to carry a bunker, you're going to play with more fear. That's a huge stress for you.

But if you improve your bunker skills and actually enjoy hitting those kinds of shots, you're not going to be thrilled if you dump your approach in the sand, but you're prepared to get yourself out if necessary. You're going to play with way more confidence because you believe you can recover from a mistake.

CHAPTER 2

How to Get Better

Without Changing Your Swing

IN THIS CHAPTER

▷ Making better strategic decisions will pay immediate dividends

▷ Pick the best strategy for your skills

▷ Managing your emotions is a fundamental part of the game

▷ How to connect with your target

▷ How to avoid interference

"A bad attitude is worse than a bad swing." — Payne Stewart

W**ITH ALL THE TIPS** in the golf magazines, books and videos out there, it's obvious that a ton of players are looking for the magic bullet that will change the mechanics of their swing.

Mechanics are certainly part of improvement, but before you dive into some of those tips—or into a lesson program—your best bet is to find the lowest hanging fruit, so to speak.

You can significantly lower your scores by ignoring your golf swing (temporarily) and making some simple adjustments to your on-course strategy and your attitude.

DECISIONS, DECISIONS

N**O MATTER** what level of player we're talking about, everybody gets upset and annoyed about leaving shots out on the course.

In the 2015 U.S. Open, Dustin Johnson was one shot off the lead on the 18th tee. He hit a perfect tee shot, and an awesome approach shot to reach the par-5 in two. But he missed a 12-foot eagle putt for the win and a four-footer for birdie that would have forced a playoff. He put a good face on it after, but three-putting is just one of the things that burns tour players up.

You have your own set of unique game characteristics—shots you like to play and shots you don't, strengths and weaknesses. How you manage those skills is a much bigger indicator of how you score than how "perfect" your shots are.

What does that mean?

Let's say we're following a twosome. Both players have the same 15 handicap, but their games couldn't be more different. One player has power, but not much control over direction. He bombs some tee shots, but one out of every three goes off the planet. He can hit some short clubs into greens, but he doesn't have a very sophisticated short game. His putting is very streaky.

The other player? He's short and relatively straight off the tee. His problem is getting to greens in regulation. He likes to hit one particular kind of short game shot, and is really good at it, and he's a good putter.

The overall scoring capability for those two players is the same, but the way they make their scores is totally different. That fact has to inform the way they choose to play the game.

When you start to break down the decisions players make on every hole—from club selection to shot selection to picking the amount of risk you want to take—some of those decisions should be clear cut for any player, regardless of handicap level.

For example, if you have a chance to pitch out into position where you can make an easy bogey, attempting a shot you can pull off one time out of ten in an effort to get on the green isn't a good choice. It's still not a good choice for a tour player who could make the shot four or five times out of ten.

Another example? Pin placements. Tour players hit the ball high and far. But even they see pin placements where it's foolish to try to jam the ball in there over a bunker or right next to a water hazard. They pick a safer route, and hit a shot to the middle of the green. They're looking to two-putt and get out of there with a par.

Those two 15-handicappers should be making the same kinds of calculations. Every pin isn't a green light. If the more powerful player has a wedge in his hand, he can consider a few more options, but if you're dealing with a close bunker that would leave you with a short-sided sand shot, you should be making the same decision as the tour player. Play it safe and for two putts. Even if you three-putt for bogey, you're probably putting a better score down on your card than if you hit it in that short-side bunker. A bunker shot to 30 feet and a three-putt later, you're making double.

The shorter 15-handicapper? He has to make decisions about putting the ball in position around the green where he can hit a shot he likes. From 200 yards away, it isn't automatically reaching for the 3-wood to try to hit it up there as close as possible—because rolling it into the bunker in front of the green and leaving a hard sand shot is much worse than being 60-90 yards out with a comfortable wedge distance.

If you didn't change anything about your decision-making besides committing to getting *out* of trouble when you get into it, you'd shave shots immediately. That means taking your punishment and getting back out into play, or, as tour players say, getting back into position.

If you hit one into the trees, getting out of trouble means pitching back to the fairway so you can play the hole "normally." Your ego might tell you you can be Seve Ballesteros, but the truth is that for every hero shot you hit, you're going to hit eight or nine that bounce off a tree and turn into a triple bogey. It's why a 20-handicapper stays a 20. The 10-handicappers are the ones who play a bad hole and salvage a bogey or double instead.

An important byproduct of improving your decision-making is that you're going to enjoy your rounds way more—because you're going to be playing your own game instead of trying to impersonate somebody else's. Have a tight par-4 at your course that eats you up? Who cares if your buddy hits a driver there. Use a hybrid or middle iron to get the ball in play and avoid making a big number.

This is also where a good PGA professional transitions from a swing instructor into the role of *coach*. It's important to be able to show players how to make better swings, but a coach should also do the important work of helping a player identify his or her weaknesses so they can be addressed. If you hate hitting downhill bunker shots, that's an important thing to know when you're picking what shot to hit into a green with bunkers on both sides—and an important thing to be working on in your practice life.

At the more advanced levels of the game, the best coaches are doing this with their students all the time. Dustin Johnson hits it plenty far. In the last few years, he and his coach, Claude Harmon III, have been working on his wedge game—and it has nothing to do with swing mechanics. Dustin hits a variety of wedge shots on the range and tries to guess the ultimate carry distance of the shot before the ball lands. They verify how well he's doing with TrackMan. That simple game has made Dustin much more aware and tuned in to his off-speed wedge shots—and he's making a ton more birdies because of it.

When Justin Leonard was growing up at Royal Oaks Country Club in Dallas, he was one of the smallest kids in his class. He never hit the ball very far, so he needed to have a lights-out short game to compete. He and his coach, Randy Smith, made sure to do a lot of work on the quality and variety of his short game shots—and dialing in his putting—so that Justin could excel with the game he had. It doesn't mean they didn't try to get him to hit it farther. But if you're not practicing the kinds of shots you see all the time on the course, you're missing a big opportunity to cut strokes and play *your* best game.

SEEING YOUR GAME CLEARLY

ONE OF THE BIG CONTRIBUTORS to bad decision-making on the course is something we all come built with automatically. Emotions are a part of golf, and the players who are able to manage their emotions the best are usually going to have the most success.

Your emotional response to a situation can be big and obvious—like feeling intense pressure over an important tee shot or a putt. Or it can be more subtle—like your attention wandering over the course of 18 holes, or playing loose and free when there's nothing on the line but cracking when somebody puts a bet on the line.

One of the cruel ironies of golf is that the less skill you have, the harder it is to control your emotions—which, in turn, makes it harder to shoot better scores. A tour player who is playing well isn't standing on the tee hoping his ball doesn't slice into the woods because it almost never does that. But for a 20-handicapper who plays with a left-to-right ball flight, the fear is real because he's seen it happen. A lot.

This is another place where a real, realistic awareness of what your game is and isn't is going to help you. Using that same example of a 20-handicapper fearing that shot going to the right, if you know your game, seeing that shot come out every once in a while isn't going to make you happy, but you know from experience that you take your lumps and move along. It isn't the end of the world.

And really, that's the secret to modulating your emotions. You condition yourself over time to put situations in realistic context. You become used to the emotions coming, and instead of trying to block them out, you process them and move on.

I can remember Tiger Woods being asked before the 2015 British Open how he kept himself from getting nervous on the course. He said he didn't. Getting nervous was part of the experience, and he embraced it. "The first tee shot, I'm nervous. I care about what I do," he said. "When I'm not nervous, that's the day I quit. That means I don't really care what I'm doing out there. I want to feel the rush and feel the nerves. It's just a question of how you handle it."

Nervousness and anger aren't bad things. And making a mistake because of them isn't bad, either. If you can embrace the nervousness and emotion, you can use it as a kind of internal challenge. Can I handle the stress of this shot? Can I come back and play a good hole after messing up this last one? That's what makes the game fun. And if you ask most of the great players, they'd tell you that exact challenge—and the feeling of accomplishing it—is the main reason they play.

Jason Day came close at a lot of different major championships before finally winning the PGA in 2015. When he got asked about how he dealt with the previous failures at other majors, he immediately said he didn't think of them as failures. He didn't win those tournaments, but he took something from the experience—and used what he learned the next time.

I love that attitude, and it's one I try to instill in all of my students. And it's something that works no matter what your goals are.

Do you want to play competitive golf—whether that means in amateur or pro tournaments or one of the flights of your club championships? Do you want to break a scoring goal? Get under 100, 90 or 80?

Either way, putting yourself in position to feel the pressure of those situations is the only way you're going to improve your ability to handle the emotions that come with them.

To handle a shot when it matters, you need to put yourself in position to hit more shots that matter. One way to do that is to always play for some kind of stakes. It doesn't have to be a bunch of money. You could play for a dollar, a drink or a cheeseburger. Just something to focus your attention and add some competitive pressure.

Outside of actual competition, there are a few ways you can build some of that emotional tolerance in your game. One is to learn how to deemphasize the value of any single shot over any of the others in a round.

You'll often hear tour players say they focused on "playing one shot at a time"—so much that it's become a cliché. But clichés are clichés because they're usually true. Those players are practicing on focusing all their energy on hitting the shot they have in front of them, then putting it away and doing it again for the next one. The net effect of that is that they let go of what happened before—good or bad. The time for evaluating a score is later, when you're signing your card or going in for a beer in the clubhouse.

Maybe the best example of this came on one of the biggest stages. Dustin Johnson had to play most of his final round at the 2016 U.S. Open under unusual uncertainty. Would he get a penalty for his ball moving on the fifth green? Instead of trying to predict what USGA officials would end up doing after his round, he focused on what he could control. "I was swinging well, and I just kept thinking, it's me and the course," he said. "I'm playing against the course, and I can't control what anyone else does."

Johnson made a great up-and-down on 17 to save par, then birdied the last hole to go four ahead of Jim Furyk, Shane Lowry and Scott Piercy. Rules officials ended up giving him a one-shot penalty for his situation on the fifth hole, but it didn't matter in relation to the final outcome.

It's obviously hard to get that level of focus with the snap of your fingers, but any amount you can improve at it—even if it's just a few shots a round to start—is going to help your performance. One way to improve is to intentionally think of your round as a combination of sharp focus and soft focus moments. You can let yourself relax, look around and chit chat with your friends for all of the time in between shots, but at a predetermined point before you play the next shot, it's time to get super focused.

Again, it will take some practice on that skill, but if, for your next round, all you did was make the conscious decision to narrow your focus 60 seconds before each shot, you would see dramatically increased performance.

Another one of my favorite techniques is something you can incorporate into your practice session tomorrow. Instead of just beating balls, or going through your regular practice sequence, spend 10 minutes of your time alternating between 60 seconds of aggressive jumping jacks or jumping rope—to get your heart rate up—and settling into your routine and hitting a shot. Try it on the putting green, too, before hitting a tricky four footer with some break. You'll quickly get a better feel for what your heart rate is doing and how that impacts your swing—and you'll be more used to the heightened emotional state you'll be in when the stakes are high.

Plus, you'll get in a little cardio!

INTERFERENCE & THE TRIP EFFECT

B EFORE WE FINISH HERE, I want to tell you one more story that will hopefully help you play your own game. One of the realities of golf is that most of the time you're going to be playing with other people. It's one of the things that makes the game so great, but it can also bring up some challenges.

You're bound to run into a playing partner that does something to potentially throw you off your game. Maybe he or she is a slow player, or has the tendency to chatter a lot—or maybe unintentionally remind you of all the times you might have struggled on a certain hole. Or maybe he or she has a swing that is really fast or awkward looking.

When these distractions come into play, you get off your game without even realizing it, which can be detrimental to your enjoyment and per-formance on the course. I call this the "Trip Effect"—and it can happen to golfers of all abilities, especially in tournament play when everyone's intensity is higher than normal. To help you recognize the warning signs, let's go through some classic examples of the "Trip Effect" so you're better prepared to handle these potential distractions on the course.

The Slowpoke

Without question, one of the biggest challenges in golf is playing with a slow player. The tendency can be to start fuming over the pace, and then hurrying your own process when it gets to your turn because you've become so impatient.

To beat this problem, start by not watching the slow player as they play. Once you hear their shot has been hit, begin your routine and play your shot. If you sense your group is holding up the course, simply let the group behind you play through, which should help bring attention to the matter. Avoid playing the role of the ranger or the professional staff with your playing partners. Your best bet is to call into the golf shop for help. They will be glad to assist, and you can spend your energy concentrating on your own game.

The Chatterbox

We've all played with players who love to tell stories. Those stories can sometimes bleed into the time you need to get ready to play a shot. If this happens (and you're trying to be part of the conversation) you'll lose your focus on the shot at hand, which usually produces a poor result. It's usually unintentional on the part of the storyteller, but sometimes an opponent is using it to throw you off your game.

If you're feeling distracted as you address the ball, simply back away from the ball and ask them to "hold that thought." On tour, you'll see players back off their shots anytime they sense a lack of focus for the shot at hand.

The Negative Talker

Unfortunately, there are a lot of folks that are never happy. They will find something wrong with the course setup, the pace of play, the food they had at the club, or some other run-of-the mill nuisance. If you get caught up listening to their negative chatter, it's easy to start your own chain of bad thinking that can take you off your game and leads to intensity management issues, especially after a poor shot.

To avoid this negative influence on your game, I'll share with you a powerful concept I've learned from Stacey Devine—who is a phenomenal physical therapist and life coach—called "What You Focus on You Amplify." With that in mind, avoid focusing on their negativity and focus your energy on the positive experiences you've had in life.

The Awkward Swing

If you're paired with a golfer that has an unusual swing, or a tempo (super fast or super slow) that doesn't match up to your game, it's often times best not to watch their swing. Sam Snead was once asked how his swing compared to Ben Hogan's, and he had an interesting thing to say: "We had similar swings but I would never watch him swing because he swung so fast it would throw off my timing."

Another scenario is you're playing with someone who has a dramatic swing flaw or an abrupt hit as they strike the ball. If you watch this action throughout the round, it can adversely affect your performance, so avoid watching these players whenever possible.

The Phone Person

Last but not least, the biggest distraction that comes into play is our phones. To play your best, you have to try to avoid checking your phone between shots or trying to play while you're on the phone. On top of that, you're killing the experience for your playing partners, especially if you leave the ringer on and you're getting calls throughout the round. Obviously, we all have the need to be connected to our family, work, and unexpected emergency situations. Having said that, do your best to disconnect with the device to connect with your playing partners and you'll have a much better experience on the course.

CHAPTER 3

How to Make More Putts

"A man who can putt is a match for anyone." — *Willie Park*

W**HEN YOUR CONSIDER** how putts vs. other shots you take during a round, it's interesting to think how little organized attention that part of the game gets from most players. I say "organized attention" because plenty of players go to the practice green and hit some putts and call it practice. But if you don't really know what's supposed to happen in a putting stroke and you aren't keeping track of how well or how poorly you're doing-or you have a putter that doesn't fit you- you aren't doing your putting game any favors. And even if you have a great putter that fits you well and a stroke that works just like it should, you won't make as many putts as you could if you don't know how to read a green correctly. This is an important conversation to have, because putting is very important to your game, and it's a place where any player can see some improvement very quickly. You don't have to turn into a professional athlete to get better, and the skills it takes to be a good putter are ones that anyone can learn.

Let's start with the basics of a putting stroke. A lot of what you read or see in videos is determined to give you "ideal" putting mechanics. You'll hear about ways to hold the putter and ways to make the club itself swing back and forth-either in an arc or straight back and straight through. If you came to me for a putting lesson, we'd get to the point where we talk about the mechanics of your stroke, but long before that, I want to see how you intuitively make a round object-the ball-move with the flat surface of the putter face.

If you're a bad putter, it's likely you don't have "touch"—the ability to make the ball go the correct distance when you putt. For example, if you have 22 feet to the hole, touch will determine how close you get the ball to the hole. You might start the ball on line, but leave the ball six feet short, or past the hole. The distance problem could be because you don't know how to make the right size stroke, your stroke timing is inconsistent, and/or you struggle with consistent contact.

Another reason many golfers struggle with putting is a poor mindset that leads to indecision, lack of confidence, and intensity management issues. Regardless of your issue(s) I don't think you need to tear down your putting stroke and start over to putt well—as long as you can follow my simple guidelines that follow to improve your physical and mental skills for putting.

1. Use a grip that works with your stroke. Whether you choose the classic reverse overlap grip, the cross-hand style that Jordan Spieth prefers, or claw grip used by Sergio Garcia, know that all are acceptable if they complement your stroke.

For example, if you like the sensation of the lead arm moving the putter back and through, the cross-hand grip is a great choice. It's also a great way to help the golfer that struggles with having his or her upper body too open at address—which makes it difficult to start the ball on line. If you like the sensation of releasing the putter like Tiger Woods, you will probably prefer a more traditional grip like the reverse overlap. If you struggle with your hands working together during the stroke, the

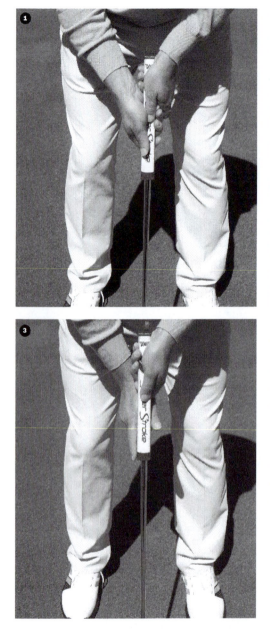

▷ You can grip the putter with either your lead hand at the top of the grip (1) or the bottom (2). On either grip, the index finger of the hand closest to you rests on top and along the pinky of the other hand (4,5). In an alternative grip like this one (3), the lower hand cradles the club with the index finger running down the side of the grip. It's great for players struggling with the yips.

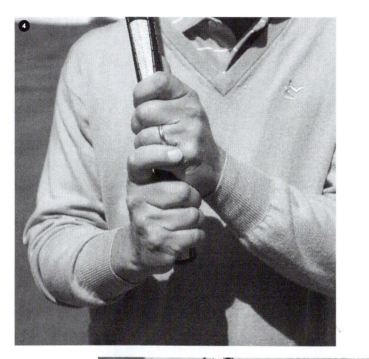

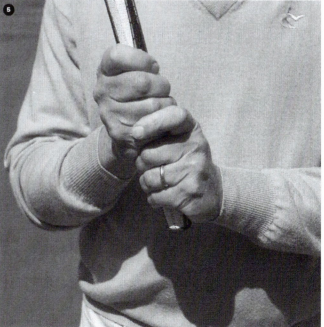

claw grip can be a big help and is worth a try.

Regardless of what you use, be sure to pick a grip size that complements your stroke and what you like to feel when you putt. For example, if you like to use your hands to sense the putter releasing, a traditional grip size is often the best option. If you want to minimize hand action, go with a bigger grip size.

2. Stand where you can see the line. How do you find your best stance? Go to the practice green and find a straight uphill putt around 10 feet from the hole. Set a ruler in front of your ball that is aimed directly at the hole. Now, set up to the ball, stay in your posture, and turn your head and follow the ruler towards the hole with your eyes. As you do this, a few things will happen. If you're in a good stance, you'll see the target. If you're seeing things left of target or right of target, it's time to make some adjustments. Start by turning or tilting your head and see if that helps things improve. You might stand up taller or bend over more to fine tune your position.

Another important consideration is ball position. Adjusting the ball forward or back in your stance can make a big difference in how you see the target—and so does how close or how far you stand from the ball. Regardless of the adjustments you need to make, having a clear view of your target is what you're after.

The most important setup fundamental is to be in a stance that lets you see your line without any visual noise. The best putters have figured this out and have a stance that lets them connect with the target and flow with their stroke. How should you stand? First and foremost, avoid getting pigeonholed with standard advice like getting your eyes over the ball. That's probably the most overrated tip in putting. You can crouch over like Dave Stockton or stand more upright like Raymond Floyd. You can stand with a square stance, an open stance, a closed stance, and have great results. What matters most is that you can see the line and can deliver the face square to your intended line at impact.

3. Improve the quality of your strike. If you're hitting the ball in the center of the face time after time, you're going to develop touch and consistency. I define a quality strike as hitting the ball in the center of the face with the right loft on the putter, and with the putter face square to where you want the ball to go. Why didn't I mention anything about the path of your stroke? Because some cool new research by my friend and fellow instructor Kevin Weeks shows that it doesn't have much to do with making the ball start on line. You can have a straight back and straight through stroke, a curved one, or one that goes outside-to-in, or inside-to-out. What matters most, is that the face is aimed at where you want it to go when you make contact with the ball. To work on this important skill, I recommend the Gate Drill which is easy to setup with just a couple tees and a ruler.

The Gate Drill.
STEP 1. Place the ball on the green 4" behind a ruler on your intended line.
STEP 2. Use two tees to form a gate that is the width of the putter.
STEP 3. Roll some putts through the gate and strive to have your putter face square to the gate as you strike the putt.

4. Develop consistent stroke timing. Regardless of the kind of stroke the best players use, you will see a commonality in their stroke tempo, which is the relationship between the backstroke and forward stroke time. For virtually every great putter, that relationship is extremely consistent, regardless of the length of putt. To track this, I recommend the Blast Motion Sensor, which lets anybody keep track of this ratio. I recently did a corporate event with Brad Faxon—who has always been regarded as one of the best putters of all time. Brad works with Blast and its founder, Michael Bentley. Looking for one main reason Brad is such a good putter? No matter what putt length he had, his timing didn't change and his distance control was impeccable.

What should your stroke time be? It depends, but the golden rule is

▷ An easy way to check your aim is to set a ruler in front of your ball aimed at the hole.
Adjust your stance until you see the line clearly. Note your position, and strive to get
into this stance and posture when you putt.

▷ Another useful drill to try is to place two tees in the green in line with the front and back edges of your putter head. Place the ball directly between the tees, and practice making strokes so that the head hits both of the tees at the same time. This will ensure solid contact with your club face square at impact.

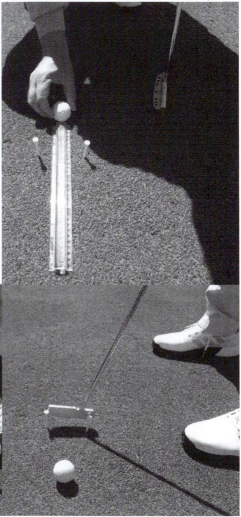

that it needs to be consistent. If you have a slower backswing time like Lydia Ko or a faster backswing time like Brandt Snedeker, your overall stroke time will be different. Regardless of what timing you prefer, strive for consistency and your putting will improve.

Another tool that works quite well for improving the cadence of your stroke is a metronome. Now a days, you can easily download a free app to use on your phone. When you launch the app, adjust the timer somewhere between 60-90 beats and find the timing that feels best for your stroke. It's a good idea to count with the beats (one, two, back, thru to find your best option). Once you find your preference, roll putts from various distances with the metronome providing auditory feedback as you putt.

As you do this, it's also a good idea to understand the relationship between your stroke length and distance the ball travels on different green speeds. An easy way to do this is to roll some test putts in a flat area on the green with a specific backswing distance in mind. Use a ruler and some tees to reference a few different backswing lengths from 4-12 inches. Be sure to use consistent stroke timing and note how far the ball rolls as you vary the length of your backswing. On medium speed greens, you'll get around 10-feet of roll with eight inches of backswing. On slower greens less, and on faster greens more. As you add more stroke length (do it in 4-6 inch increments) you'll see the ball travel a greater distance if your stroke timing remains consistent.

5. Dial in distance control. On tour, Jordan Spieth is in a league of his own when it comes to making putts over 20 feet. Why is that? His speed is near perfect on every putt and the hole gets in the way. If they don't go in, he's simply tapping in instead of grinding on a four footer that most golfers face after their first putt. Although statistically it's unlikely you'll make a bunch of putts from long range, you'll improve your three-putt avoidance and feel less stressed on the greens if you practice my Speed Zone Drill.

The Speed Zone Drill.

Use three alignment sticks to define the speed zone which in this case rewards putts that finish within a couple feet of the hole.

To test your touch, putt from 15, 30, 45, and 60 feet. Set markers at each distance for easy reference and roll several putts from each station.

Now it's time for a touch challenge. See if you can get, challenge yourself to get three-in-a-row in the speed zone (one from each distance).

As you do this on a regular basis, you'll improve your touch and sense of distance—which will translate into lower scores. One more suggestion on this—challenge a friend to compete with as you do this drill and you'll push each other to improve this important skill.

6. Improve Your Make Percentage on Short Putts. Putting from close range is one of the most nerve-wracking parts of the game for most golfers because they rarely practice this skill. Conversely, tour players spend countless hours every week making putts from short range—even though they make 95% of their putts from three feet and 85% from four feet.

To improve your short putting skills, practice my Runway Drill. To do this, take two alignment sticks and form a runway to the hole that is slightly wider than the width of the cup. Set the ball four feet from the hole on a reasonably straight putt that goes slightly uphill. Now it's time to make some putts and build confidence on your short putting skills by rolling putts through the runway and into the hole. As you do this, strive to make 9 out of 10 and you'll be beating the tour average from four feet!

Looking for a bigger challenge? Move back to 8-feet and see if you can make 6 putts out of 10. Do this and you will beat the tour average of 50%. When you go through this exercise, you'll appreciate the physical and mental endurance it takes to be a good putter. If you compete in tournaments, be sure to make your practice sessions end with a challenge and you'll be better prepared to handle the pressure in tournament play .

▷ Place a yardstick outside your line and stick tees in the ground at four-inch intervals. Now you can see how a putt's distance corresponds with the length of your backswing.

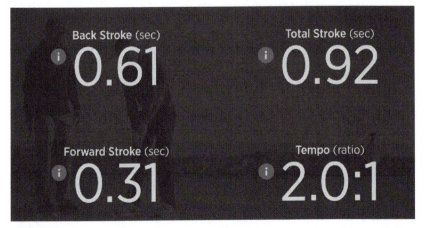

▷ The Blast Motion sensor sends you information about your stroke and tempo (*left*).

▷ Build a "speed zone" with alignment sticks that rewards you for leaving putts within a few feet of the hole. Practice from distances ranging from 15-60 feet and strive to have all your putts finish in the zone.

SECRETS TO EFFECTIVE GREEN READING

F ALL YOU WORRIED ABOUT WAS SPEED, you'd still be a decent
putter, because you'd still be within a few feet of the hole just by getting
the speed right and a read that was somewhere in the neighborhood of
the hole. But if you want to make more putts, you do need to get the read
right. And green reading is a definite skill.

How do you read greens?

If you play at the same course regularly, you probably use your memory to recall similar putts that you have faced in the past. But how is this
going to work when you play another course with unfamiliar greens if you
rely on memory? Probably not well.

Most golfers are green guessing instead of green reading.

To accurately read greens, you need a process. Even people who have
a specific process for reading greens don't often do it exactly right. You
can walk around your ball and the hole and check things from different
angles, but if you don't know what you're looking for, you're not doing
much besides adding doubt to your mind.

The goal—obviously—is to predict break, so you can aim appro-
priately. But your eyes can deceive you. Let's say you're a golfer that
visualizes the apex (the high point on the curve) when you putt.
Although this may seem logical, it accounts for less than 50% of the
break. What about the rest?

That's where my good friend and AimPoint Founder Mark Sweeney
comes into to play. Mark is one of the smartest guys I've met in the golf
business, and has revolutionized the green reading process with his green
reading system that you see used on all major tours.

When you see a tour player holding fingers out in front and looking
with one eye at potential break in a putt, you're seeing somebody use
AimPoint.

In 2009, I was fortunate to refine my green reading skills and knowledge by becoming the first AimPoint Certified Instructor in the Mid-

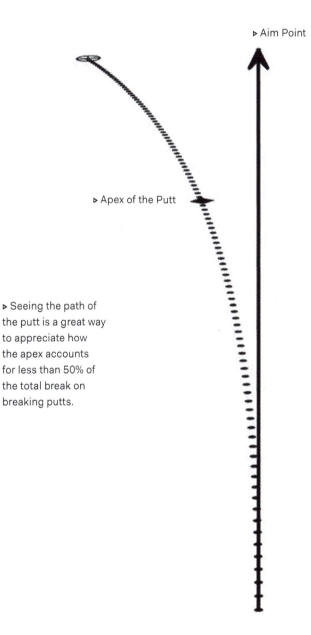

▷ Aim Point

▷ Apex of the Putt

▷ Seeing the path of
the putt is a great way
to appreciate how
the apex accounts
for less than 50% of
the total break on
breaking putts.

Atlantic Region. Since then, I've taught thousands of students how to read greens with greater precision which has helped their putting and approach shot strategies during play.

To improve your green reading skills, I've put together a quick geography lesson on the most common green shapes you'll play on the course. Then I'll share with you a green reading process to help you gather the right information in a timely manner and help you with your on course strategy.

PRIMARY GREEN SHAPES

ONE OF THE COOLEST THINGS about golf is that every hole is different. For example, you could be out playing a course with small greens that have a limited number of hole locations that rarely change, or you could be playing greens that are so big you could hit a lob wedge from the front of the green to the back.

No matter what the size, understanding the primary green shapes will help you make better reads and strategic decisions.

Before the advancements in drainage technology, architects built most greens with a prevailing slope. The green usually tilted in one direction, with a high side and a low side. This design was great for helping water

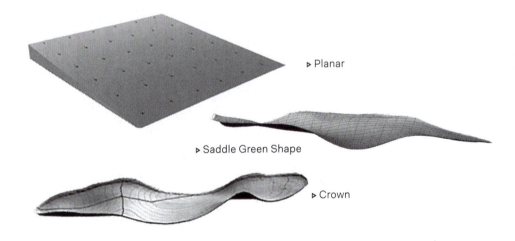

▷ Planar

▷ Saddle Green Shape

▷ Crown

flow off the green. This type of green shape is often described as "planar" (one plane), and most golfers are able to read break direction on this type of green. The primary challenge on planar greens is that they feature steeper slopes that cause the ball to break far more than most golfers will ever play. They also make it harder to make speed adjustments on uphill and downhill putts. With that, do your best to keep your ball under the hole and avoid missing the green on the short side (where you have very little green to work with) and you'll save strokes.

Now let's talk about the other two primary green shapes that come into play—crowns and saddles.

Crowns are great for dividing greens, and feature an uphill and down-hill section that is connected by a flatter section. In most cases the flat section (the top of the crown) is where you'll have putts with minimal break. Most golfers over-read their putts in this area. If you're putting from longer range and crossing a crown, you'll experience a putt that double-breaks due to changing slope.

Be sure to judge the slope direction in the middle of the putt to determine the overall break direction in this scenario. Having said that, the bigger challenge is judging the speed on longer putts since you are putting through multiple slopes. Be sure to practice my Speed Zone Drill in a crowned section to improve this skill.

Saddles are easy to see as they feature two high sides (let's call them humps) that form a half-pipe shape that is easy to see. Although the humps feature steep slopes, the area between them is a wide, flat section that runs off the green into a low area.

If you see a pin placement in a saddle, do your best to keep your approach shots within the saddle and you'll have a fairly straight putt. If you miss the green in the low area, it's generally an easy up and down since you're heading straight uphill.

THE GREEN READING PROCESS

NOW THAT YOU HAVE a better understanding of green shapes, it's time to refine your green reading process. It starts when you approach the green and look for obvious clues in the path of your putt before you mark your ball. This saves a tremendous amount of time and keeps you engaged in the in the present so you can make a decisive and objective read in under 45 seconds.

STEP 1. On the way to your ball, head to the middle section of your putt and stand on the low side to avoid walking in your line.

STEP 2. Assess the slope characteristics in this section along with the overall distance of the putt.

STEP3. Head back to your ball and visualize the type of putt you want to play.

As you do this, go with your first impressions as you assess the putt. When you watch players struggling with their putting, it starts with their inability to make a decisive read.

Why does this happen?

Usually, it's because they don't have a reliable process to predict break, and they're getting lost in details that may or may not matter.

Another common mistake is watching another player putting from a different position and thinking you need to change your read based on their outcome. If you watch the best putters, they often look away while someone else is putting to avoid this distraction.

Beyond that, I've listed below some basic guidelines to help you improve your green reading skills. Call them rules of thumb. If you follow this advice and still struggle, be sure to take an AimPoint Green Reading Class from a certified instructor. To find a class in your area, visit AimPointGolf.com.

▷ The green-reading process starts before you get to your ball. Begin your read as you walk onto the green, getting the overall feel for the green's inclination (1). Then walk to the low side of the break, halfway between the ball and the hole, to get your first direct read (2). Stand behind your ball and visualize the putt (3).

RULES OF THUMB

THERE ARE MORE STRAIGHT PUTTS THEN YOU THINK. If you see
more than one break in a putt, or it goes over a crown, the tendency
will be for the putt to play relatively straight. This happens because of
off-setting breaks that occur as the slope changes on longer putts. Resist
the temptation to over-read the break and concentrate more on getting
the speed right. Avoid giving the hole away on putts that are less than
four feet unless you are putting across a heavy side slope. The ball doesn't
have much time to break and you'll avoid those painful lip outs if stay
within the runway on your short putts.

—**Downhill putts break more than uphill ones.** A main factor in break
is time. If you have a downhill putt, the ball leaves at a slower speed than
a putt of the same length going uphill. When a putt takes more time, it
has more time to break.

—**Don't get tricked by bodies of water.** This one is a response to an old
rule of thumb- the one where if a green has a pond next to it, putts will
break towards the water. They might, but it's random. The body of water
isn't necessarily where the slope direction is heading in the path of your
putt. Read the putt as you normally would and don't be surprised if it
breaks away from the water.

—**Beware of the come-backer.** Just because a ball broke from right to
left on the way to the hole doesn't mean it will break left to right from
the other side, if you missed it long. All approaches to a given hole have
their own slope characteristics. Don't assume anything and be sure to go
through your normal green reading routine carefully each time.

—**Grain is your friend.** First and foremost, think of grain as a
frictional component. If the grain is growing towards you, the putt will

play slower and break less. If it's heading in the direction of your putt, the putt will play faster and have more break. In most cases, grain direction equals slope direction except in rare instances. You can often times see this when you look at the light and dark areas on a green. The light areas are the downhill direction, and the dark areas are the uphill direction relative to your position. On flatter greens, the color change can be a big help for determining slope direction and green speed.

—**Make time to improve your craft.** In the 20 minutes before you play a round, you can go through a process that will get you putting better when it counts. Start by rolling putts from 20 or 30 feet on a relatively flat green surface not to a hole but a tee, working only on solid contact and speed. Next, go around a hole and make putts from two feet as if you were visiting the stations of a clock. Start at two feet and then go out to three feet, with the goal of making six putts in a row before you move on. Finish with a series of 30- and 40-footers to a specific hole, taking the time to read each putt and concentrate on lagging well so you can two-putt each. Now you're ready.

THE MIND OF A GOOD PUTTER

ONCE YOU'VE MADE THE READ, you're work isn't done. You need to translate that read from your eyes and your mind into your setup and stroke. Trace the specific path you see the ball taking with your eyes from the ball to the hole. This visual and mental preview is the mechanism that lets you convert thoughts into an athletic response when you putt. That's a big part of what separates great putters from just OK ones—the ability to gather the best information and translate it into a confident stroke. Maybe it isn't a perfect one, but making a confident stroke on a line you've committed to is way, way better than making a tentative stroke on a perfect line.

When you pick your line and make a committed stroke, watch the putt roll out and accept the outcome. It isn't good or bad—and it isn't a triumph or tragedy if the ball went in or didn't.

When you start to second-guess yourself and get emotional, nervous or angry, your mind tends to fill up with lots of chatter regarding the past or future outcomes. That makes it even *harder* to make a good stroke.

Under pressure, thinking clearly is a huge challenge for any golfer. Trust your instincts, avoid indecision, and manage your intensity level. Sometimes you need to try less and sometimes you need laser like focus to play your best. Here are some of my favorite quotes that reinforce the mindset of champion golfers:

I never hit a shot, not even in practice, without having a very sharp, in-focus picture of it in my head. It's like a color movie. First I 'see' where I want it to finish, nice and white and sitting up high on the bright green grass. Then the scene quickly changes and I 'see' the ball going there: its path, trajectory, and shape, even its behavior on landing. Then there is this sort of fadeout, and the next scene shows me making the kind of swing that will turn the previous images to reality. —JACK NICKLAUS

I always feel pressure. If you don't feel nervous, that means you don't care about how you play. I care about how I perform. I've always said the day I'm not nervous playing is the day I quit. —TIGER WOODS

The most important shot in golf is the next one. —BEN HOGAN

The more important the putt, the less I try. —BRAD FAXON

The smaller the target, the sharper the athlete's focus, the better his concentration, and the better the results.
—BOB ROTELLA, GOLF IS NOT A GAME OF PERFECT

ROLLING THE RIGHT PUTTER

P**UTTERS ARE FUNNY.** Players can have a hot streak of putting and get attached to a club that might not be the right fit for them in the technical sense, but they're so comfortable looking at it that it stays in the bag.

Other players cycle putters in and out every weekend, looking for the magic bullet that will make them make more putts.

Why is it that some putters look and feel so great, while others just don't work at all? I hate to tell you this, but it has nothing to do with magic. Putters work or don't work because they fit you physically, and they have a head shape and weighting that suits your eye and stroke. You might have lucked into the right putter by accident, but it happens more often when you get fit specifically for your body and stroke characteristics.

Take putter length for example. Most stock putters come 35 inches long. Is it because a 35-inch putters fits a player of average height? Nope. It's because 35" putters were the right length to not fall through the dividers in golf bags.

Maybe a 35-inch putter is right for you. But it's just as likely that you need one 32 or 38 inches long. The right putter length complements your stroke, and makes it more comfortable for you to stand over the ball. If you like having your arms straighter at address, you'll need a shorter putter. Phil Mickelson uses a 32" putter even though he's more than 6 feet tall. David Toms, on the other hand, is a shorter guy, but putts with bent elbows. He uses a 35" putter.

When it comes to the actual style of the head, you want to use something that you can look down and feel comfortable, not confused. You should feel confident aiming the putter and the weight of the putter should feel good in your hands.

Beyond that, be sure to see a qualified fitter who can fine tune the loft on the putter to match your strike. If you tend to add loft or decrease loft, making adjustments can be extremely helpful to improve the quality of roll you produce when you putt.

▷ Setup to ball with a strong base of support to swing the putter.
Your arms should hang where you have the best feel for your stroke.

▶ If you prefer straighter arms at address, you'll want to go with a shorter putter. Like more bend in your elbows? Go with a longer putter. Regardless of what style you choose, go with what gives you consistent stroking timing and a quality strike on your putts.

CHAPTER 4

How to Hit It More Solid

*"The sole purpose of the golf swing is to produce a correct
repetitive impact. The method employed is of no significance as long
as it is correct and repetitive." — John Jacobs*

SOCIAL MEDIA is great, but one of my least favorite things
about it is the way it tends to reduce discussions about
technique into two-dimensional conversations, videos and photographs
of certain swing positions.

Don't get me wrong. I love looking at swings, and I'll happily watch
hours of video of different tour players and students hitting balls. I'm not
trying to say that there's nothing to be learned from videos or photographs.

But.

I'll often get an email from a student (or a potential student) with a
video attached, and the player wants to hear what I think about his or her
swing motion. But unless I can see what the ball is doing, and also get a
sense for how consistently the player is doing what he or she wants to do
with the ball, I'm missing a big piece of what's required to do my job.

Swing models are fine, and everybody can enjoy watching Adam
Scott, Dustin Johnson or Lydia Ko make a golf swing. But those are three
professional athletes with different bodies, different capabilities—and
unlimited time to practice. What every player needs is a plan for what's
possible for *his* or *her* body. With the body and capabilities you have, you

could well be better off with a totally different swing shape than a particular tour player. It will look different, but that's completely OK.

As players like Dustin Johnson, Jordan Spieth, Lydia Ko and even Jim Furyk have proven, there are lots of different ways to be good at this game. Those ways are certainly informed by swing mechanics and good instruction, but the instruction comes in the form of making the pieces work together for what you can do.

My goal here is to establish some building blocks for you to be able to make solid contact on your shots, and to make the ball do what you want it to do with swing capabilities you have. It's not a template or a method. It's a way of identifying what pieces could work the best for you.

Let's start with some basics.

"Angle" is a word I use a lot at the beginning of my time with my students, because it's a fundamental concept that informs a lot of what a player is trying to do. To hit solid shots, the club needs to come into the ground at the right angle for the shot you want to hit. My good friend and mentor, Jim Hardy describes this as the +/- system of Impact and Ball Flight correction.

If you're struggling to hit solid shots, you can put yourself into one of two loose categories depending on which clubs in your bag give you more trouble. You're either striking the ball with too much angle, or with not enough.

If you have no trouble taking divots and you notice those divots are on the deep side, you're probably somebody who has more than enough angle when you strike the ball. You may have issues hitting your wedges consistent distances or hitting shots when the ball is sitting up, and you're probably erratic with your driver. Some of your ball flight misses are probably pop-ups, straight pulls, slices and shots that launch extremely low. If this sounds like your game, your angle at impact is too steep.

If you're the player who rarely takes a divot, you're probably most happy hitting driver—and you don't like hitting long irons when the ball isn't on a tee. Hitting out of the rough is a big challenge, and your ball flight misses are thin and fat, pushes and hooks because your angle at impact is too shallow.

Regardless if you're too steep or two shallow, your improvement process needs to start with fixing your angle issue to improve your club delivery so you can make solid contact on your shots.

As you can imagine, there are lots and lots of different swing shapes and shot shapes out there. How you address what you do right and wrong should start with the predominant ball flight you're seeing on your bad shots. I can already hear some of you thinking to yourself that you hit a variety of different bad shots. What I'm talking about here is your *most common* miss. I'm going to take you through a list of different shot shapes and give you some basic ideas to implement if you want to make those shapes more neutral.

THE HOOK

As I MENTIONED ABOVE, people with a shallow angle tend to struggle with left curves because the face is sweeping around through the ball. If you're a player who hits a hook, it means that you're approaching the ball at a shallow angle and the face is closing too quickly relative to the club path. An important step to take is to create a little bit more swing angle down into the ground to support the face. Instead of focusing on the face being too closed at contact—which makes you tend to swing even more to the right—the focus should be directing the club down and left.

I use three simple drills to give students the right feel. Place a towel six inches behind the ball, and hit some practice shots making sure to avoid hitting the towel before you get to the ball. You can also find a downhill lie on the range and hit a small bucket of balls while striking the ball with the club moving down the slope. If you don't, you'll hit very thin shots. The third is more of an adjustment than a drill. Adding pressure to your left thumb can be a big help in stabilizing the clubface and eliminating the hook. To do this, grip the club as you normally would, but increase the right hand lifeline pressure on top of the left thumb.

When doing this, it's helpful to remove the right index finger and thumb to accentuate this feeling and get both hands working as a unit. Now it's time to hit some shots with this sensation. When you do it correctly, you'll hear the sweet sound of solid contact and you might even see a fade! By the way, this was one of Ben Hogan's favorite drills to improve the grip and eliminate the hook.

▷ The Towel Drill

▷ Adding pressure to your left thumb can be a big help in stabilizing the clubface and eliminating the hook.

THE STRAIGHT PULL

T'S IMPORTANT to differentiate the straight pull from the hook, because many players lump them together as the same mistake even though they're generated by very different issues. The player who hits a straight pull is making solid contact with the ball, which means the angle to the ground is good. Most people would say it's the best feeling shot they hit. But the path and face are going to the left as you strike the ball.

You need to make a path adjustment. It could be as simple as moving the ball a little back into your stance and working with feedback on the start direction of your shots. To do this, take two driveway sticks or alignment rods and set up a gate 20 feet down range. Put the inside stick right on the target line, and set the outside stick so that it's four feet to the right. Go back and hit a small bucket of balls so that your shots start by going through that gate. Visualize each ball heading through that window before you swing, and feel like the face of the club is aimed just to the right of that window at your setup.

Another great way to feel this is to take a water bottle and put it just past where you'd impact the ball, but to the inside of the target line, an inch inside the heel of the club. If you can make full swings without hitting the bottle, you're moving your swing direction to the right. You can also ask your teacher or clubfitter to check out your clubs for lie angle. Players with clubs that are too upright often feel like they stripe the ball, but end up with this pull. You can also check to make sure your ball position hasn't drifted too far up, or that your shoulders and clubface aren't tweaked left of the target at address.

THE LOW LEFT SHOT

F YOU'RE HITTING shots that go both low and left and they aren't hit solidly, you have a hat trick of issues that need to be addressed. You need to shift the bottom of your swing so that you have less angle into the ground, a swing direction that is more to the right, and a clubface that isn't closing so dramatically through impact.

To fix this, we need to give you some awareness of sweeping the ball off the turf as you strike the ball. To do this, tee up ten balls, fairly high off the ground. Grab your 7-iron and strike the balls without breaking the tees. To help your chances, put a straw in your mouth and keep it pointing at the back of the ball as you make your swing. After doing a few sets of this drill, find an uphill lie on the practice tee and hit some shots with the sensation of swinging up the slope. When you get the hang of it, you'll feel a totally different impact as you strike the ball. If you're still crashing the club into the ground, be sure to check out my "Down the Wall Drill" on page 55 and my "Side Bend Drill" on page 81 for more assistance.

THE BIG RIGHT MISS

WITHOUT QUESTION, the most common ball flight miss for most amateurs is the slice. It's a weak shot that often misses the target short and right, and comes from wiping across the ball with an open clubface. In terms of angle, slicers can be steep or shallow. If you're a steep slicer, your divots are deep, and point left of where the ball finishes. If you're a shallow slicer, you rarely take a divot, and you're often told you never get off your back foot. To fix a slice, it's always a good idea to check your left hand grip as most slicers have the club too much in the palm of their hand. To fix this, move the handle of the club into the base of your fingers. When you do this, it will be in your hand very much where you'd carry a piece of heavy luggage. It's also important that the you check the placement of your V (the crease between your thumb and index finger should point at your right shoulder).

Assuming your grip is reasonably correct, it's time to check your upper body alignment at address. If you're like most slicers, your body lines are well left of the target which makes it easy to deliver the club from out to in. Let's square you up and make a couple tweaks to your swing to eliminate the slice.

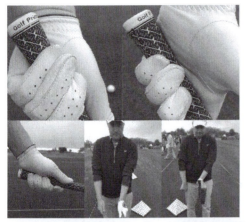

▷ Here's a look at the grip so you can appreciate poor placement (in the palm) vs. proper placement in the fingers. It's also important to check the position of your "V" in your left hand (the crease between your thumb and index finger) should be pointing towards your right shoulder.

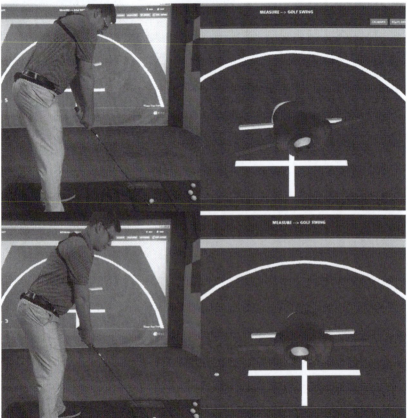

▷ When your upper body alignment is well left of the target, it is important to square things up to better your chances. Here's a great visual of this in 3D on K-Vest.

Now that you've fixed your setup, it's important to route your arms and the club around your body to help eliminate the slice. To learn this motion, hold your left wrist with your right hand and guide your left arm into the backswing, across your chest. As you do this, you'll feel some pressure across your chest and a nice turn with your upper and lower body. If your range of motion permits, continue this motion until your left shoulder touches your chin. This is great indicator of the top of the backswing that includes a nice windup.

Now let's give you the right feel from the top swing to impact to eliminate the big right miss with my "Down the Wall Drill". The Down the Wall Drill is a great way to learn the correct motion of the club from the

▷ Down the Wall Drill

top of the swing to impact. When doing this drill stand 18 - 24 inches from the wall and practice the start of your downswing by feeling the club glide down the wall. As you do this, you will learn what you need to feel to stop swinging over the top and slicing your shots.

If you move outward with the club in a classic "over the top" move, you'll feel the club immediately moving away from the wall. When you do this, your body spins out and you tend to fall back through impact—which is a common fault for a shallow slicer. If you're steep slicer, feel how much your right side moves downward in the first part of your downswing and you'll get rid of those steep impacts.

The wall drill also teaches you how to unlock your wrists and gets energy out to the club as you strike the ball. Most importantly, it will get you out of lead wrist extension which leads to a wide open club face at impact, and the big right miss. When you use the wall, you'll be amazed at how much earlier and easier the club releases and squares to your path, which will dramatically improve your ball-striking.

THE PUSHER

THE PUSH TENDS TO BE a "good player" miss. It's a shot that starts right and stays to the right, but is hit pretty solid and doesn't curve much. It's not that bad of a shot, and it usually tends to go approximately the right distance. Many tour players hit what I would call and intentional push—a shot that starts right of target and stays right."

If you don't like this ball flight, it's probably because you're trying to hit more of a draw—usually to get more distance. Start by checking your grip. Make sure the V's in both hands point towards your right shoulder. If they aren't, adjust accordingly and your push should turn into a push draw. Another adjustment to consider, is to move the ball a fraction more forward in your stance to reduce the in-to-out path tendency that causes the push. But don't get too radical with your changes. A miss without a lot of curve or variation in distance is a valuable miss to have!

SHANKS

THE SHANK (or "the dreaded shank," I should say) is one of the most alarming shots in golf. It takes off abruptly to the right and puts anyone standing to that side in danger. Although you might think the club is extremely open at impact when this happens, it's not the case! The shank happens because you're striking the ball in the neck of the club. When this happens, your club will sound broken. Despite this, most golfers think the shank is from hitting the toe side of the club.

To fix the shank, we need help you find the center of the face by eliminating your mistake that is causing you to hit the ball with the neck of the club. Generally speaking, the shank usually presents itself with players that make one of the following mistakes.

1) Swinging excessively in-to-out to offset a closed clubface and/or excessive hip thrust.

2) Swinging excessively out-to-in from losing balance towards your toes from an outward arm swing and/or excessive spine flexion through-out the swing.

If your shanks are coming from a club path problem, the water bottle drill on page 58 will be a big help. If your shanks are coming from excessive hip thrust, the plunger drill on page 59 is a great way to fix your problem.

Even if you don't shank, it's important to recognize the cause and the sound of this shot for safety reasons. If you're playing with someone that has this shot in his or her arsenal, don't stand to the right or walk ahead of them when they are hitting irons, especially at the range! If you hear that broken sound off the club, remember what Lee Warner (affectionally known as "Bulkhead") tells his playing partners: "Don't Crowd the Plate!"

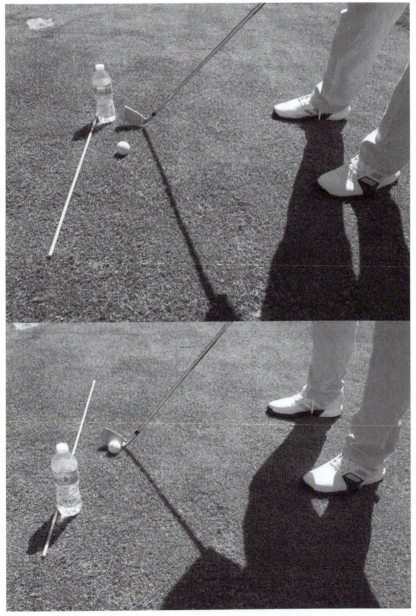

▷ A simple practice station with a water bottle will help you adjust your club path, pre and post impact. To avoid an out-to-in club delivery, place the water bottle just outside the ball your hitting, and 6 inches behind the ball. To avoid an excessive in-to-out release, set the water bottle 6 inches past the ball and just outside the target line.

▷ An excellent drill to work on start direction, is the gate drill. Place two alignment sticks in the ground, 4 feet apart and 10 yards down the target line. Practice hitting shots through the gate and your ball striking will improve.

▷ Excessive hip thrust can lead to a variety of ball flight misses that include thin, fat, pushes, and shanks. My plunger drill will help you curb this mistake. Position it on the ground so the stem provides feedback if you thrust towards the ball. The stem should be along your toe line, and centered in your stance.

THE SHORT GAME

LOVE TEACHING short game, and it's a special passion of mine. It could easily fill an entire book if you want to know the intricacies of each flavor of shot. But the vast majority of all golfers coming in for lessons or corporate events really are looking for the basic shots they can count on during play. Simply put, they want to know how to get the ball on the green and have a *reasonable chance to one-putt or two-putt.*

I'll work on lots of different variations of short game shots with my regular students—who come in with a certain level of skill. But any player will have a better short game if he or she starts with the three shots I'm about to show you and grows things from there. If you can hit these three shots, you're going to be able to handle nine out of 10 short game situations you face. And the 10th? That's going to be a hard shot no matter what you do, and trying one of these three isn't going to be any worse that trying to pull off a miracle with some other technique.

We're going to learn the basic low, medium and high shots that will give you the kind of coverage you need for a complete short game. The main difference between the shots? They each require a different angle into the ground as you strike the ball. For low shots, your club should strike the ball with minimal angle (much the way you strike a putt) to ensure you contact the side of the ball. As you need to produce more height, you're going to come in with more speed and angle, to slide the club under the ball. And when you need to get out of a bad lie, I'll show you how to escape without hitting the ball first. It's chunk-and-run—the one jack-of-all-trades shot you can use out of most trouble situations.

One of the main reasons players struggle with short game is because they pick the wrong kind of angle for the shot they need—or they pick the wrong club. To help you with this, let's go through how to play low, medium, and high shots around the green. You'll learn how to play these shots successfully with just a few clubs and avoid the pitfalls that add unnecessary strokes to your score."

LOW SHOTS

BEFORE WE START in on the technique you need to hit a low chip with an iron, I need to remind you of a very valuable short game weapon in your bag.

Your putter.

In club golf, there can be a stigma attached to using a putter from off the green, but it's something the best players in the world do all the time. At the 2014 U.S. Open, Martin Kaymer used his putter with great success whenever he needed a low shot around the green, and he went on to win the championship. Although putting from off the green isn't a flashy shot, you're already familiar with the stroke. You might not hit a perfect shot, but you'll eliminate stubbing the ball and other misses that add unnecessary strokes to your score.

If you need more airtime on a low shot, your next best bet is playing a standard chip with your 8-iron. One of my favorite descriptions of this shot is by my good friend and mentor Jim Hardy, who describes the chip as a "skipping putt." To play this shot, position the ball where you can clip the ball off the turf with club traveling low to the ground on both sides of the swing. How far will the ball go? It depends on the surface and how hard you swing. Generally speaking, your 8-iron will roll out three times the carry distance assuming normal green speed and firmness. If you want less roll out, simply chip with a club that has more loft. Looking for more? Use a club with less loft.

Another low shot worth exploring is the hybrid chip. You'll see lots of tour players using this shot when they don't want any chance of getting the club stuck in the ground. This is especially helpful when the ball is sitting down in the grass around collar of the green, into the grain on Bermuda grass, and on upslopes near the green. To play the low shot with the hybrid, raise the handle as you set up to the ball so you can stand closer, and make your regular chipping swing. The heel of the club might feel up at address—which is perfectly fine for playing this shot.

◁ The hybrid chip is a great choice for low shots around the green, especially in greenside rough where the hybrid will glide through grass as you strike the ball.

▷ A great way to practice clipping your chips off the ground is to place the ball on a low tee and focus on clean contact as you strike the ball. To help this, keep the club

▷ LOW SHOTS

Regardless of what club you choose to chip with, be sure to keep the club low to the ground on both sides of the swing with no attempt to help the ball into the air. Let the loft on the club do it's job and you'll make solid contact on your low shots around the green.

◁ 8-Iron Chip

low to the ground on both sides of the ball with a slight arc and your chipping will greatly improve.

From there, you'll need to give yourself some reps to get comfortable with how the ball comes off the face and rolls out. Once you get the hang of it, you'll find this to be the easiest club to chip with and it very well might become your go to club for low shots around the green.

Regardless of what low shot you select, it's always important to watch the roll out on your shots for future reference. Equally important is remembering that your swing needs to be calibrated to the landing zone and not the hole. If you struggle hitting your low shots a short distance, chances are you're gripping the club with too much pressure. To help with this, imagine your grip is wrapped in bubble wrap and you don't want to burst a bubble when you make your swing.

MEDIUM AND HIGH SHOTS

O PLAY medium shots or high shots around the green, you'll want to use your sand or gap wedge. (Yes, you can use your lob wedge, but I'd tell you to get skilled with your sand and gap wedge before trying to use the least forgiving club in your bag.) These shots are commonly referred to as pitch shots and they are played with a "U" Shaped Swing. With this action, your club will glide along the ground as you strike the ball. To do this, follow these guidelines and you'll hit soft landing pitch shots around the green.

MEDIUM SHOTS

ET UP to the ball with your club slightly open and the ball positioned slightly forward of middle in your stance. Your feet should be a comfortable width, where you feel balanced for the shot. It's also important that your arms are hanging comfortably and ready to swing. As you make the backswing, the club goes up with a fold of your right arm and some wrist action as you make your turn. As you change directions, the goal is to strike the bottom of the ball with the club gliding along the turf just before and after impact. When this is done correctly, you'll see the right arm and the shaft in line post impact. You'll also see the ball launches virtually at the same speed as the club, which is ideal for medium trajectory shots.

HIGH SHOTS

To play high shots around the green, you'll need the right lie for the club to glide under the ball. The high shot works well from the first cut of rough, the fairway, uphill lies, and when the ball is above your feet. Unless you're a tour player or an elite amateur player, DO NOT attempt this shot off extremely tight lies, downhill lies, or when the ball is below your feet. Assuming you have the right lie to play this shot, here are some guidelines for your setup and swing.

To play the high shot, you'll need to add more loft, more speed, and more glide as you strike the ball. To do this, we need to make a couple adjustments to your setup and lengthen your swing. In your setup, you'll want to open the club a bit more, and lower the shaft angle by lowering your hands. Both of these adjustments will add loft and bounce angle which is vital for gliding the club under the ball at impact.

With these adjustments, you'll need to adjust your posture for a stronger base of support to make this swing and glide the club under the ball. To do this, take a wider stance, add some foot flare, and more knee flex relative to your normal stance. Now the fun part! Taking a big swing that produces a high soft shot. To do this, take some practice swings near the ball that are at least 80% of your full swing length and speed. As you do this, pay attention to where the club strikes the turf and position the ball in your stance accordingly.

When this shot is played correctly, the club speed is higher than the ball speed and you'll see the ball launch high and land soft on the greens. To put things in perspective, a 20-yard high shot requires the same speed you'd use to play a 60-yard shot from the fairway with your sand wedge.

▷ **MEDIUM AND HIGH SHOTS**
around the green are best played
with the sand or lob wedge. Be sure
to set up to the ball with the club
slighly open, and the ball slightly
forward of center in your stance.
Notice how the right arm and shaft
are in line past impact, with the loft
of the club pointing towards the sky.

▷ Your pitch shot will fly high and soft when you let the
right arm and the club work together through impact with
the loft of the club pointing skyward into the finish.

▷ Bunker shots—and shots from deep grass—get much easier when you understand how to use the bounce on the bottom of the club. Make this part hit the ground vs. the sharper leading edge.

▷ To practice using the bounce, place a nickel an inch behind the ball and hit shots making sure to hit the nickel first. If you dig in, you'll never get to the ball.

BUNKER SHOTS

F YOU'RE like most golfers, you've had mixed results from sand, rang-ing from leaving it in the bunker to flying it over the green and out of play—which makes it a scary shot. Worse than that, you've heard the pros say it's an easy shot. Just hit a few inches behind the ball.

In general, that's a sound concept, but I would say that the majority of poor bunker players hit too far behind the ball. To improve your bunker shots, let's refine your understanding of how your club should enter and exit the sand. Tee a ball up in the bunker and push it down so that the bottom of the ball just barely touches the surface of the sand. Now make your swing with the intention of knocking the tee out from under the ball. When done correctly, you'll see the club strikes closer to the ball and exits the sand well past the ball.

To set up, stand to the ball with a wide stance, plenty of knee flex, and a lower shaft angle. It's a good idea to flare your feet to help you squat into this lower position which you'll see the best players doing when they setup to play bunker shots. As you get into this stance, the club will ap-pear more lofted and open when you lower the handle. This is an ideal stance for playing bunker shots and any high shot where you want the club to slide under and past the ball.

Now that you're set up correctly, it's important to remember that you need a swing that will have enough speed to cover a typical greenside bunker distance. That means swinging as if you were hitting a 30-40 yard wedge shot from the fairway—or even more for longer bunker shots.

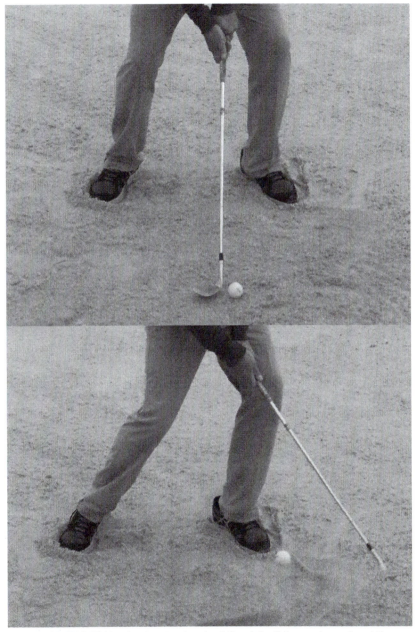

▷ **BUNKER SHOTS** Here's a great example of the club gliding under and past the ball on a bunker shot. Notice how the left knee stays flexed well past impact which is an often overlooked fundamental on bunker shots.

▸ To hit successful bunker shots, you need a swing that generates at least 30-MPH to get the club gliding under and past the ball. Notice how the club face is skyward

throughout the bottom of the swing and the knees stay bent well past impact.
Do this and you'll escape the bunkers with greater consistency and save strokes!

THE CHUNK-AND-RUN

N OT EVERY LIE is going to be perfect, and the beauty of this shot is you can use it from deep grass and other sketchy lies around the green. You can even use it in the bunker when the ball is sitting down, or when you want the ball to land with minimal spin and roll out across the green.

The chunk and run is best described as a crash landing of the club behind the ball that plows the ball out of these tough lies. Since you aren't actually hitting the ball first, you won't get much spin, so expect some roll out when the ball lands on green. With that you'll need to pick a landing zone, well before the hole to account for the rollout.

To play this shot successfully, you need to strike the ball with enough angle to penetrate the area behind the ball and keep the club low to the ground through impact—very much like a punch shot. I use my sand wedge for most of these shots, but a gap wedge works well if you have a long distance to cover. Because so much of this shot is dependent on the quality of the lie, you want to take some practice swings near your ball in a similar lie (except in the sand) to get a feel for the resistance you'll encounter on shot. The worse the lie, the firmer your grip needs to be to handle the resistance you'll encounter on the way to the ball.

Once you pick a landing zone that gives you room to roll the ball out to your target, set up to the ball with 70% of your weight on your left side and position the ball where you can plow through the junk on the way to the ball. The handle of the club should be slightly ahead of the ball to encourage an early set of your wrists in the backswing so you have plenty of angle to deliver the club down and through the junk on the way to the ball. Remember to finish low to the ground and the club without any attempt to lift the ball into the air. Do this, and you'll escape those tough lies around the green.

▷ CHUNK AND RUN

There are many variations of the chunk and run that will get you out of difficult situations around the green. Remember to let the club do the work and don't worry about a bad finish. The junk between the club and the ball will tend to grab the club as you strike the ball.

CHAPTER 5

How to Get Off the Tee

"Don't ever try to sell me on that line, 'Drive for show and putt for dough' — to my mind, the most important shot in Golf is the drive. Hit it well, and you have a jump on the hole, and edge on your opponent. Hit it poorly, and you'll be scrambling all the way to the green." — Greg Norman

Y OU'LL HEAR AND READ all kinds of different "secrets" to getting the most out of your potential in the game. And there are certainly strokes to be saved by improving your short game, putting, and iron play. But at any level, it's really hard to score if you can't drive the ball in play. If you're constantly recovering from bad positions off the tee, you're putting a ton of pressure on the rest of your game. Your iron play has to be better, and your short game and putting have to be spot on for it to go well. I bet if you think of your last truly bad round, it came because you were wild off the tee and took some penalty shots or punch outs to get back into play.

No matter if you're a tour player or a 20-handicapper, driving the ball in play with enough distance is a huge advantage that puts you in position to score. Keep in mind that in play doesn't always mean you're in the fairway. It simply means you have a reasonable chance to reach the green on your approach shot—which could be from the first cut in the rough, a fairway bunker or even an opening in the trees. There are plenty of golfers who hit lots of fairways but lack distance. Because of this, they rarely hit greens in regulation, which means they are battling to make bogey or worse on most holes.

On tour, proof of this concept comes from comparing the traditional golf stat of fairways hit with a more modern one, strokes gained driving, developed by Dr. Mark Broadie. Broadie's stats have completely changed the way players track their games—and link distance with driving location to establish exactly what factors lead to improved or reduced scoring chances.

HOW TO FIND A DRIVER THAT FITS YOU

BEFORE YOU START making changes to your driver swing, we need to talk about the club you have in your hand. I see a lot of new students who come in with a $500 driver that barely has the plastic off the head. And after watching several swings it's clear the club doesn't fit them.

For a lot of people, the shaft might be the wrong length, flex or design for their launch conditions. Another common mistake is that lots of folks immediately adjust the driver head to a draw setting because they slice— and that moves the center of gravity towards the heel. Although this can be magic for some golfers, it can be tragic for the player who strikes his or her shots toward the toe of the club. And by the way, most slicers hit the toe.

If you don't get fit for your driver in terms of length, loft, shaft flex and head weight adjustment, you're making the job of hitting solid shots way harder than it has to be. With that, invest in a driver fitting and get the right equipment to maximize your potential off the tee.

First and foremost, be sure to seek a qualified, experienced club fitter that uses measurement technology (Trackman, GEARs, Foresight, Flightscope) and has a matrix of heads and shafts from various manufacturers to evaluate your launch conditions. It's also extremely important to hit premium balls when testing clubs to get reliable data and verify you're playing the right ball on the course.

With respect to the data, you'll want to see the numbers that relate to your launch conditions: club and ball speed, spin and launch, and the peak height and landing angle on your shots. As you go through this process, you'll see your club speed will change the least of all the numbers, but the ball speed will definitely improve when you get the spin and launch dialed in. You'll also see how the peak height and landing angle can make a huge difference in terms of how much roll you get on your drives.

Another indicator that helps determine how well a club is performing is the "Smash Factor" which is the relationship between ball speed and club speed. A good rule of thumb? You want to go through a fitting and at the end of it, have a driver that is producing a consistent ball flight with a smash factor of 1.43 or higher. What is the maximum smash factor you can get? It's 1.52 based on the U.S.G.A limits on the club face.

As you go through the fitting process, you might find the right driver after just a few swings, or it might take 50 or more. Either way, be sure to pace yourself, because hitting drivers for an hour is tougher than you think. Lastly, be sure to avoid drivers that produce inconsistent results even though you might hit them extremely well at times.

Once you have the right club in your hand, it's time to investigate your impact point tendencies. Thousands of dollars of teaching technology is great but you can get some answers right away with change from a $10 bill at CVS. Go get a can of foot powder spray or a black dry-erase marker and cover the face of your driver. Hit some shots and check the marks on the face after a series of shots. The goal is to have a consistent impact point in the center of the clubface. If you're hitting the same spot consistently but that spot isn't in the middle of the face, you're just an equipment tweak away from better drives.

If your strike is towards the heel, it's important to go with a driver that allows you to move the center of gravity in that direction. Another option you might want to consider is a shorter driver length—which has worked great for Rickie Fowler and Jimmy Walker. Or, you can simply set up towards the toe side of the driver like Zach Johnson and give it a rip. If your impact point is towards the toe, move the center of gravity in that direction, and adjust the lie angle setting to a more upright position. A classic mistake with adjustable drivers is moving the center of gravity away from your impact point. If you do this, you'll lose clubface stability and the club will under-perform. This happens to a lot of slicers, who move the center of gravity towards the heel to the "draw" setting, which doesn't help when their impact point is towards the toe. Instead of making that mistake, adjust the loft settings. On most drivers, adding loft will make it easier to draw the ball and decreasing loft makes it easier to fade the ball.

If your driver offers an adjustment for spin, keep it neutral until you've found the right setting for the face and loft. From there, make subtle adjustments and you'll find your best setting.

If your launch monitor data shows you're a high-spin player, chances are you have a negative attack angle and a driver with too much loft. This often occurs with players that hit their drivers with a steep club delivery and have higher club speeds. Be sure to look for deeper faced driver with less loft and a low spin shaft option. If you're a low-spin player, you likely deliver the club with a shallow attack angle and you need more loft on the driver to avoid a ball flight that dives to the ground, especially if your club speed is under 80-mph. It's also a good idea to seek a lighter shaft with a softer tip section to help increase your launch and spin.

Now that we've discussed the impact point across the face, it's also important to discuss the vertical impact point which relates to how high or low you strike the ball in the club face. If you tend to hit the ball high in the face, chances are your club delivery is on the steep side and you need to use a lower tee. If you hit the ball low in the face, your club delivery is too shallow and you should use a higher tee.

WHAT YOU CAN LEARN FROM THE BEST DRIVERS OF THE BALL

FOR MORE THAN 20 YEARS, I've filmed thousands of tour players hitting tee shots to study their swing styles, ball flight patterns and on-course strategy. As I began this journey, golf instruction was very much in the model mode of a specific set of positions that you should be in as you swung the club. Although this seemed like a logical approach, it was clear there were endless combinations of swing styles used by the best players in the game. Despite this, the best drivers of the ball share a common set of fundamentals with their on-course strategy and how they setup and strike the ball.

Fundamental #1: Maximize Your Landing Area

Before any tee shot, pick a target that suits your ball flight and strategy for the hole. For example, if your ball flight is left-to-right, aim at the left side of the fairway and that will help you maximize the width of the fairway. One of the best drivers of all time is Colin Montgomerie, who plays a sizable fade on his tee shots. He aims down the left side of the fairway and uses the entire width of the fairway with this approach. If you play a fade or a slice and you're aiming into the middle of the fairway, you've shrunk the landing area and made the shot play much tougher than it should. If you play a draw or a hook, simply aim down the right side. How far off center should you aim? The golden rule is never aim where a straight shot hurts you.

Fundamental #2: Take an Athletic Stance

The best drivers of the ball set up to their shots so they can deliver the club to the ball with a wide arc at the bottom of the swing. To help with this, set the ball just inside your left heel with your feet at least shoulder width apart. Equally important is a strong base of support from the feet up—which comes from a balance of knee and hip bend, and enough spine bend to let your arms hang comfortably before you swing.

Fundamental #3: Side Bend at Address and Impact

Although there are many swing styles, the most common trait you'll see with the best players on the driver swing is that they never get ahead of the ball during the swing. To help with this, setup to the ball with your spine tilted slightly away from the target. During the swing, your spine motion is ever changing, just like any athletic motion. To produce a wide arc at the bottom of your swing, you'll need some additional side bend that helps transition the club and your body into the hitting zone. To feel this, place your right hand on the right side of your pelvis after you take your stance. Now drive your right hip and leg towards your left leg and you'll notice the side bend increasing as you make this move. You'll also feel what it is like to have the right hip driving into a firm left side which is a key move for hitting solid tee shots.

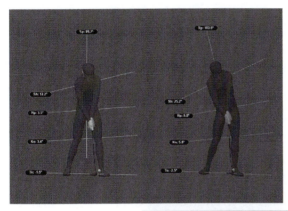

▷ GEARs 3D Motion Analysis is a great way to examine side bend and other metrics during the swing.

▷ Most golfers who tend to look at their swing from the down the line perspective forget to check their swing from face on. This is especially important with respect to side bend at address and impact you'll see the best drivers of the ball. To better understand this relationship, grip the club with your left hand and place your right hand on the right side of your pelvis. Now, drive your right side into your left side and sense your right side bend increasing as you make this move. You'll also feel the right side driving into a firm left side which is a key move for hitting solid tee shots.

Fundamental #4: Make an Uninhibited Swing

More than any shot in golf, speed is essential to hit solid tee shots. Stay aggressive with your swing by letting the club release freely through the ball. A great way to feel a free flowing release with plenty of speed is to practice swinging your driver upside down and above the ground. As you do this, listen for a nice swish and enjoy the feeling of an uninhibited swing.

Fundamental #5: Develop a Power Move
That Matches Your Swing

If you're looking to hit longer drives, be sure to find a power move that matches your swing. Throughout the history of the game, the best players have used different swing keys to hit their longest drives. Jack Nicklaus would drive his legs to compliment his upright swing, and Ben Hogan would clear his hips to match his flat swing. If you watch today's longest hitters, you'll see players swinging so hard their feet are barely on the ground as they strike the ball—like my student Kyle Berkshire, who hit a 433-yard drive at the 2017 World Long Drive Championship. I can assure you he's not thinking of jumping off the ground, but he does have a power move of accelerating his left shoulder up and back as he smashes his drives. What should your power move be? It depends. My advice is to keep it simple, athletic, and complementary to your swing.

All of these movement patterns come from the ground reaction forces that are present in all athletic activities. You can't see them, but they can be measured with the Swing Catalyst 3D Motion Plate. Fortunately, I have one in my teaching studio, and have captured thousands of swings to examine these patterns on a wide range of golfers. From the data, and my collaboration with Hall of Fame Teacher Mike Adams and Swing Catalyst's Director of Research, Dr. Scott Lynn, we've found some distinct patterns to help golfers maximize their power potential—which we share in a book, video series and presentations around the world. You can find more information about it at my website, BernieNajar.com

▷ One of my favorite drills to feel a free flowing swing with the driver is to flip the club upside down and make swings above the ground. Do it right and you'll hear it whistle.

▷ The right tee height will get you the most benefit of the driver's technology. Teeing it low, so the ball is in line with the face (*top*), will produce shots with more backspin. Tee it half a ball higher than the face (*bottom*) to launch it high and far.

▷ The proper tee height is relative to your impact point tendency. If you hit the ball high in the face, go with a low tee height. If you hit the ball low in the face, go with a high tee height. Remember, the best way to determine this is by spraying your driver with foot powder spray and note the results.

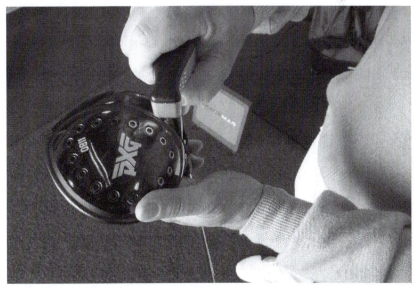

▷ Most drivers today are super adjustable to help you dial in a more consistent shot shape. You're losing out if you don't get the help of a teacher or fitter to get yours tuned in.

Fundamental #6: Develop a Go-To Shot
For Demanding Tee Shots

When you find yourself on a hole with trouble on both sides, it's critical to get the ball in play with a shot you can trust. During his prime, Tiger Woods went with his "Stinger" tee shot, which he used with great success on some of the tightest holes on tour. Other players will play a sizable fade to get the ball in play, or a big draw if that suits their eye. How can you hit these shots? It's actually not as hard as you think.

To play a stinger, move the ball in the center of your stance and tee it low. Be sure to stay centered over the ball throughout the swing and you'll produce a penetrating ball flight that rolls like crazy on firm fairways. Keep in mind the stinger is best played with a driver or a long iron. Avoid trying this shot with lofted fairway metals or hybrids as they not going to work as well.

To play a fade, move your ball position up in your stance and grip the club so that the face is slightly open. From there, aim down the left side of the fairway and let it rip! This strategy has been used by many top players, and was Jack Nicklaus' go-to shot off the tee.

To play a draw, go with a fairway metal, or hybrid as they are much easier to draw than a driver. Move the ball slightly back your normal ball position and grip the club so that the face is slightly closed. From there, aim and swing down the right side of the fairway and you'll see a nice draw flight.

Fundamental 7: What To Do When The Driver Isn't Working

Anyone who has played golf has had rounds where the driver isn't going where they want. It makes for a tough round of golf because you are constantly out of position. Although this is extremely frustrating, the best players have incredible discipline when this happens. They will either go to a shot they can get into play—even if it isn't pretty—or they will not hit driver until they sort things out after the round.

CHAPTER 6

How to Take a Lesson

IN THIS CHAPTER

▷ Work with a teacher who has had success with similar students

▷ Technology is a great tool as long as you have context for the numbers

▷ Take advantage of learning opportunities to improve your game

"Don't be too proud to take lessons. I'm not." — Jack Nicklaus

F YOU'RE COMMITTED to improving your game, the best way to do that is to get a golf lesson. But many people make the commitment to take lessons but they don't get the most out of the experience right away because they didn't come in with the right mindset.

That's like expecting to go to a movie and being taken to a concert instead. The concert could be terrific, but you might struggle to get your head around the change in your plan.

My favorite new students are the ones who come in with a well-rounded knowledge base and clear expectations. I'm not expecting them to know what's wrong with their swings—after all, that's why they're coming for a lesson. But if they've done some homework on me and know what I'm about, and they are clear where they want to be with their game, we're starting in the right place.

One of the most common questions I get from friends in different parts of the country who are looking for a regular teacher is about technology. Does a teacher have to have a lot of diagnostic gear to really know what's going on? Do I have to go to some high-tech studio just get a good lesson?

I'm lucky to have one of the most technologically advanced studios in North America here at Caves Valley, but I'd be the first person to say that technology isn't absolutely essential to improvement. You can get a good lesson from someone on the driving range with nothing more than experienced set of eyes and ears to diagnose and correct ball flight. But what the technology does—in the right hands—is make the diagnostic process more efficient. If I put you on my GEARS 3D measuring system, there are things I'm going to be able to see right away that might not be so easy to catch with a naked eye. And when you have the measuring tools that can show exactly what a player is doing, it's easy for me to reinforce with the student the progress we're making.

Take TrackMan as an example. If you came in with a very steep, out-to-in swing, your TrackMan numbers would clearly show this. As we made some improvements, you'd see those numbers start to change. Even if we didn't get to the ultimate destination, you'd see that we were going in the right direction.

The other benefit I get as a teacher who uses technology is that the technology has informed my eyes over the years. When I see you make a certain movement pattern, it's probably matching one I've seen while using my force plates, GEARS or launch monitors. We'll be able to get to the root cause of your issues a little faster.

I will say that some of the criticism of technology in teaching is valid in that uncontrolled information can overwhelm even the sharpest student. If a teacher doesn't give you some context for all of the information coming your way—and pick which information to share at a given time—it can be like drinking from a fire hose. It isn't a contest to see who can lay the most information onto a student. But even identifying your biggest problem isn't what's going to make you better. You have to get the right diagnosis, the right prescription and then you have to connect with the advice that gets you where you need to be.

How should you actually choose a teacher? I think it comes down to a few variables. The first is that you want to work with a teacher who has had success with players who fit the same pattern as you. If you're a junior player who wants to get a college scholarship, a scratch player who wants to win the club championship or a 20-handicapper who doesn't have a huge amount of time to practice, you want to a teacher who understands those advantages and limitations and knows how to work with you.

Another important variable is a good personality match. If you're a super detail oriented person who wants a lot of technical information, you're going to be frustrated by a teacher that stands back and watches you hit a lot of balls without saying anything. The opposite is equally true. You might like to get a quiet piece of advice here and there, but you'll be driven up the wall by a teacher who is bringing the instruction fast and furious. You can see some of this at the tour level, when players move between instructors. When Tiger Woods moved to Sean Foley, I'm sure part of it was because Sean talked about things in a different way than Hank Haney did. Sean was a guy Tiger's own age who could talk about more than just the golf swing. When you look at Mike Bender and Zach Johnson working together, it just makes sense. They're both extremely analytical, hard-working guys. When you work with Mike, you know what's on his menu every day. He has a lot of drills and practice stations, and some players really respond to that. Contrast that with Butch Harmon, who might spend three quarters of the lesson telling stories and making you feel good and the rest of the time sneaking in a tip or two. Both ways are great, as long as the player and teacher match.

A third element—and one that gets overlooked a lot—is scheduling. If you're interested in frequent lessons, you need to pick a teacher that can accommodate that—and fit within your budget. If you're a weekend player who wants a checkup once a month, the same holds true in the other direction. You don't want to build a relationship with a teacher that is interested in getting you to the practice tee weekly for intensive sessions.

Regardless of a teacher's style or the terminology or technology they use, a good teacher will be able to give you simple, direct solutions for the main problems in your game, and be able to explain to you the why behind the problems and the solutions he or she is offering.

When I start with new students, I'm very interested to hear how they assess their own swing, and then I like to take them through some skills testing to see how their assessment matches what they really do. Many times, players think they're better or worse at a certain skill than they really are. The assessment gives you a very specific report card. You might hit your clubs very straight, but you don't have much difference in yardage between your 6-iron and 7-iron. Or you hit your sand wedge with 20 yards difference in distances from one shot to the next.

The tendency during those evaluations is to grind away and try to impress the teacher with what you can do—or make excuses why you aren't hitting certain shots. But really, there's no upside to trying to trick the teacher. First off, we know. When you make some swings, we can tell what kinds of shots you usually hit. Second, we're on the same team, and the faster I can get a handle on what you really do when you're out on the course, the faster you can get better.

Let's talk about the difference between what a good lesson looks like and what a less successful one looks like. You might think that the quality of the shots you're hitting at the beginning of the lesson vs. the end of one is the main consideration, but that's really only a relatively small piece.

In a good lesson, a player comes in with an open mind—but isn't a blank slate. He or she has a clear idea of what he or she wants to improve, and can give details about what those bad shots look like. Speaking up is very useful: "Here's what I'm noticing in my game—I'm having a hard time getting up and down from bunkers," or "This is where I'm struggling...My tee shots are a big problem because they're going low and left."

Throughout the lesson, we're then able to work on things to improve their ability to hit the shot they want to hit—and ultimately test their ability to recreate that shot time after time. That means it's a blend of teaching (giving new information) and coaching (helping a student use what they know).

For example, when a student comes to me and talks about having a problem with his driver, we start by discussing what that actually looks like on the course. Is it inconsistency in direction? Lack of distance? One particular bad shot that shows up at the wrong time? The fix is obviously particular to that player's problem, but my overall goal is to give them both the tools to do better stuff with their swing but also improving their awareness of the warning signs that lead up to those misses. When that shot starts to crop up on the range, or out of the course, what can that player do to make an adjustment that works until they have a chance to come to the mechanic (so to speak) for a lesson?

And at the end of it, the player leaves the lesson with a playbook for what they need to do in between visits to incorporate what we've talked about. They go and do what they've been asked to do, because ultimately they need to have ownership in the process for it to work.

The contrast with a bad lesson is pretty striking. Instead of being an open conversation between two people, it becomes one-sided—in one direction or the other. Either the teacher is telling the student a laundry list of things to do, or the student is rattling off a long list of what they want to have happen. (That can also turn into a problem when parents get over-involved in a child's lesson. It can be tempting to interrupt when you hear something you aren't sure about, but it's better to let the lesson play out and address any concerns privately, afterward.) Often times, this is a matter of misaligned communication and expectations. The student doesn't come in with a specific idea of what they want to accomplish, and the teacher starts taking him or her down a road they don't necessarily want to go.

Sometimes a lesson will get derailed by the common distractions that have become so much a part of everyday life. The student could be constantly checking a phone for text messages, or show up late and distracted because of a work or family problem. Those things happen, but you're obviously going to get a better experience if you come in open, ready to learn and focused on the task at hand. It's obviously no better when the teacher is answering calls or leaving the practice area to have a conversation while your lesson is going on. It's a two-way commitment to sharing and learning.

I'll often get a question from a student about how long I think it will take to get "better." That's a hard question to answer, because it depends on your definition of better. Relative to ball flight, if you have a bad shot that curves wildly off line, you should see a reduction in the size of your miss fairly quickly assuming your teacher is on the right fix and you understand what to do. This doesn't mean you're necessarily fixed, but you are certainly on the right path to improvement. At the same time, if you keep experiencing the same miss patterns and don't see some improvement, you and your teacher need to try a different solution. My mentor, Jim Hardy is adamant about the "Next Ball Better" in this scenario which has been a great influence on my approach to ball flight correction.

You can do several things to make sure the improvements you're seeing stay in your game over the long term. First, you can ask your teacher to make you a short video summary of each lesson you take, recapping the main points and reinforcing the "homework" assignments you have in between lessons. (Be sure to store the video on your phone for easy reference). That way, you can be sure you're following the right prescription. The other thing to consider is taking at least one playing lesson. A teacher can see so much more of your game—and how it looks in the wild—when you're out on the golf course and not on the practice range. Hitting shots in a controlled environment from consistent lies is different than doing it on a golf hole when the score counts—and it will help you to give your teacher some first-person insight. A nine-hole playing lesson will not only show your teacher what you do, but it will give you a chance to get some helpful insight on some of the game's softer skills—like strategy and shot selection.

Even when you've done everything your teacher has asked and your swing has made some progress, there may come a time when you feel like you need to make a change. How do you know when it's time? If you're hearing a lot of the same things from your teacher but it isn't helping you

▷ There are many different types of lessons such as one the course, on the green, group sessions and one-on-one. As Tom Friedman says, "The best lessons are a true collaboration between the teacher and the student. If you come in empty, you leave empty!"

make changes to your ball flight, it might be time. Students and teachers disconnect for lots of reasons—from philosophical ones to scheduling issues. Sometimes it's as simple as needing a different opinion. That's OK, and it's nothing to shy away from.

You might be feeling great about the general state of your swing, but you want to add to your knowledge base. Just like in the medical community, there are some great specialists in teaching who can help you with a particular part of your game even if you're happy with your full swing instructor. Spending time with a specialist like Dave Stockton or James Sieckmann to learn more about the short game is so valuable, and there are so many great mental coaches, like Dr. Rick Jensen. There are also plenty of great group learning opportunities at clinics, schools and resorts around the country. A good teacher will encourage you to go out and find that information and not be threatened by it—because the goal has to be getting you happy and satisfied with your game!

In the end, the goal isn't to create a swing that looks just like Adam Scott's—or anybody else's. It's to improve your ball control. Everybody wants to look good in the video, but this isn't a beauty pageant. It isn't about swing positions, and it isn't about posing over shots. You're looking for predictability about where your ball is going, and the confidence to use all of your skills and tools out on the course, when it counts.

The right teacher can make that job easier, more fun and more interesting.

CHAPTER 7

How to Make Sure You Have

The Right Equipment

"By buying clubs you can't buy a game, but improperly fitted clubs will certainly be detrimental to your swing and game. If you want to play better golf, get properly fit!"
— *Wade Heintzelman, Golf Digest Top-100 Fitter*

EVERYBODY LOVES NEW EQUIPMENT, but how do you know exactly what you should be swinging? And how good do you have to be before it's time to get a fitting? There's so much help available to any player now, and it only takes an hour or two to get it sorted. How should you go about it? We're going to answer those questions and a lot more of them here.

It's a subject that's very close to my heart. I've taken a lot of pride in my clubfitting over the years, and the technology I've installed in my teaching studio—a GEARS 3D system, TrackMan and Swing Catalyst force plates—is just as important for fitting clubs as it is for teaching lessons. And I'm fortunate to be able to work with PXG as one of their first club professionals.

Most players get really excited when they see new equipment. A new driver might promise 10 or 15 more yards, while new irons are supposed to make even bad mishits fly pretty straight. And who doesn't want to find a putter that will get you making everything?

But one of the fascinating things about the subject of equipment is that as enthusiastic as a lot of players are about new gear, many of them don't take the step to make sure the gear fits their game.

Take iron sets as an example.

You can go on a website for any major manufacturer and order a set built to "standard" specs. But what does "standard" mean, and who does it really fit? When you measure a set of "standard" PXG irons and compare them to "standard" Callaways or TaylorMades, the specs aren't the same. The clubs have different lengths, shafts, lofts and lie angles. If you happen to be an average-size player with average-length arms who swings at a speed that happens to match the shafts in the irons you buy, you can have some success. In my experience, about three out of ten people I fit could reasonably use "standard" clubs.

If you're one those seven out of 10? You're going to get way, way more benefit from all the technology in modern irons and woods if you get those clubs tuned to what you actually do.

To see for yourself, coat the face of your 7-iron with the ink from a dry-erase marker. (Don't worry...it wipes right off.) Now hit a sequence of four or five balls. Are you hitting the ball in the center of the face, or consistently off the heel or toe? If you're hitting the ball consistently in the same place, but that place isn't the center of the face, your clubs don't fit correctly.

You can do the same exercise with the driver to see where you're hitting it on the face. Consistency is great, but you also need to squeeze as much performance out of the combination of shaft and head as you can. If you have a driver with adjustable weights in the head, you have a ton of different possibilities. But the shaft is the piece that gets overlooked the most. The length, stiffness, weight and bend characteristics of a driver shaft are going to have a giant impact on how far and how consistently you hit it. If you get a stock shaft from one of the major manufacturers, you might get lucky. You'll also probably be leaving 10 or 15 yards in the fitter's studio. It pays to get the weight configuration and other specs right.

What shaft is the right one? It depends on a lot of factors. But it's undeniable that in your irons and driver, you can be flushing shots and not be getting the most out of your clubs. You're using the engine of the club to its maximum potential, but you just don't have the right engine. That can mean, like I said 10 to 15 yards with the driver and five to 10 yards per club with your irons. That could be a two- or three-club difference in what you're using for an approach shot. Think that might have an impact on how close you hit it?

If you're not getting everything out of the club, does it mean the shaft in the club is lousy, or that the head is terrible? Not at all. Stock shafts are designed to appeal to the broadest audience. They're usually mid-launch and mid-spin, which is great for some players. But if you need more (or less) height or more (or less) spin, there are better choices.

Another really common issue I see is players migrating between sets of irons and drivers with the same shaft or same lie angle "because that's what I've always hit." Even if you had a lot of good years with those Dynamic Gold S300 shafts and heads bent two degrees upright, it doesn't mean that those are the exact best shaft for you. And maybe as your game has changed through the years there's a better choice. Plus, heads and shafts work differently together—especially in drivers. You might put the same shaft from your trusty driver into a new head and not get the same result.

My first piece of advice is to see a qualified, experienced club fitter that understands the impact and ball flight characteristics you are trying to achieve on your shots. The vast majority of top fitters use measurement technology to optimize your launch conditions so you select the right clubs for your game. It's also really important to hit golf balls that are similar to what you play during a fitting. You'll be amazed at the difference in shot data when you hit premium balls vs. range balls.

You need to be able to go somewhere where those options can be explored.

And what exactly makes a good clubfitter?

My friend Wade Heintzelman is one of the best I know. I met Wade in high school, and we've been talking equipment ever since. He knows what makes a great club—but more importantly, he knows what type of club would be the best fit for the player he's fitting which is so important! Using the newest technology to go with his 40 plus years of fitting experience, he understands the intricacies of the fitting process.

For example, let's say you're a low ball hitter and your mid to long irons tend to go the same distance. He won't load your bag with clubs that produce the same results which is a waste of your potential! Instead, he might build you a few hybrids or fairway woods with the same loft but alter the shaft length to produce the ball flight and distances you need in your bag. At the same time, if you're a high ball hitter, he might go with stronger lofts to dial in your distances.

THE FITTING PROCESS

D URING THE FITTING, there are a few checkpoints you can watch for to make sure you're heading in the right direction. Beyond fitting for your body and swing type, it's important for the fitter to be tuning your set makeup correctly.

As you work your way through your set, there comes a point when you're not getting significant carry from one club to the next. That's the point where you need to transition to hybrids or fairway woods. There's no shame in that happening in clubs as short as a 6-iron. The goal is to get optimal launch and good distance gaps between all your clubs.

On the other side of the bag, your wedges are often another area that most people have the wrong lofts and bounce angle for their games. Too often, I see players with too many wedges which leads to indecision on the course. This happens because a number of manufacturers have gone to incredibly strong lofts that leave a huge gap (sometimes 13 degrees) between the pitching wedge and the traditional sand wedge loft. Although their might be a huge gap, it's foolish to have two gap wedges in the bag that are rarely used around the green, or a strong lofted sand wedge that makes short game shots tough to execute.

If you end up with room for an extra club in the bag, another utility club can be a great asset for specialty shots vs. carrying a wedge you seldom use. To make life easier around the greens, go with a sand wedge loft of 54-56 degrees and a gap wedge loft of 48-50 degrees. If you go with a high loft wedge, which by the way is one of the hardest clubs to play in your bag, stick to 58-60 degrees. With respect to bounce angle, it's best to have more bounce on your sand wedge (10-14 Degrees) and less on a high loft wedge (4-8 Degrees) assuming you have proper technique around the green. On your gap wedge, you should go with at least 10 degrees of bounce and don't be afraid to go with 14 degrees if you take deep divots in the fairway.

If you struggle with bunker shots, your technique is often the problem, but having the right wedge design can make a big difference. If you play in soft, beach-like sand, a sand wedge with a wide sole and plenty of bounce will make those shots a lot easier. At the same time, a sand wedge with a narrow sole and low bounce will work easier on firm, wet sand. An experienced fitter will help you with selecting the right wedge for the conditions you play in that complements your swing technique on short game shots.

I've heard teachers and fitters say that a player is better off having more wedges in the bag and less long clubs or hybrids, but I actually go the other way on that. A vast majority of players can hit any shot you'd need around the green with a standard 56-degree sand wedge. A 60-degree is a specialty club for skilled players. If you can play with a sand wedge, gap wedge and 56, that leaves you room for another hybrid or lofted fairway wood that can solve a lot of long distance problems for you.

When you get to our driver fitting, the numbers tell the story. The fitter should be using a ball flight monitor to measure your club and ball speed, launch and spin, your landing angle, your impact point tendencies, and the consistency of your carry distances.

Keep in mind the best combination is not always the one that gave you the longest drive of the fitting session. You want your driver to be a club you can get into play with reasonable consistency and fit the conditions you play in most of the time. If you play on firm fairways, going with a less lofted driver can help you get more roll, but you'll lose some carry distance. If you play on soft fairways, focus on maximizing your carry distance since you won't get much roll. Above all, please do not make the mistake of buying a driver in a fitting where these data points are not measured.

Before you get excited and run out for your iron or driver fitting, don't forget about the club you use more than any other in the bag. People get attached to their putter because they've used it for a lot of years and made a lot of putts with it, but there's no question that a putter fitting can get a club in your hand that makes that part of the game significantly easier.

Putters should be fit to your size and posture, the kind of stroke you use, and to how you process your target visually. The kinds of alignment aids on certain putters are going to work better for you than those on other ones. These factors are a big reason why certain putters just feel good when you set up with them, and you seem to make more putts. It's because they fit. Why not go find out exactly why, and make sure you're using the best tool?

The stuff I'm talking about here isn't something you go out and do once and forget about for a decade. Taking care of your game is a lot like taking care of your car. If you do it right and regularly, the maintenance is relatively inexpensive. Wait around and things can get catastrophic.

If you're a recreational player that plays 15 times a year, at minimum you need to change your grips once a season. Before your season, you should take your clubs to get checked at the fitter for loft and lie. If you're hitting balls at the range off mats, the impact changes playing specs of your clubs over time. They can literally get bent out of shape, and a good fitter will be able to tweak them back for you.

It's totally reasonable to get four or five good seasons out of a set of irons. Beyond that, you're going to want to check for new technology and make sure your shafts are still working for you. Your game might be better than it was, or maybe you're getting a little older and have lost some speed. Either way, a tune up can help.

With drivers, technology changes much faster—both in heads and shafts. You want to get on a launch monitor with a clubfitter about every 18 months to make sure there isn't something significantly better than what you're swinging. It doesn't mean you automatically have to make a change, but knowing where you stand is important. You want to make sure your swing is still interacting with the club and the ball the same as it has.

For serious players who play more than **30 times a year**, practice a lot, and play competitively, you need to be even more aware of what's happening with your clubs. You want to check them twice a year for changes in lie angle and potential wear in the grooves. Tour players and competitive amateurs who hit a lot of sand shots go through a sand wedge every six to eight months, because the sand blasts the face and softens the grooves—which will make the ball roll up the face more instead of grab, which affects carry distance and backspin. You can also beat up the bounce on the bottom of the club pretty good hitting from sand or firm turf. Irons will probably last you two seasons, but you'll start to see some deterioration in how you can control the ball's spin.

Talking about tour players brings up an interesting point about fitting. It probably seems like a tour player's game is super far away from yours—and it is. But don't think that because you aren't shooting scores around par you aren't "good enough" to get fit for clubs.

There's no question that you need to have some semblance of a game for fitting to give you a full benefit. If you can't hit the same place on the face more than once out of ten shots with an iron, it's going to be hard for me (or any other fitter) to get you perfectly tuned in. But no matter what level you play, you're going to get some benefit out of a fitting. As you improve, the benefit just grows because the tuning can be so much more exact.

If you were a beginner and you came to see me, I'd want to make sure you were in clubs that were long enough for you had had the appropriate shaft stiffness and grip thickness. I'd also want to make sure the soles on the bottom of your irons worked for you. The wider the sole, the more forgiveness you're going to have when you hit the ground a little bit too early.

Players always ask me if I fit to the swing they have, or if I fit to the swing I'm trying to teach somebody into. The answer is, it depends. If you're a low handicap player, we're going to be able to make some tweaks to your gear that you'll adjust to pretty quickly. If you're a 25-handicap, I'll want to fit you to what you're doing now, and we can make adjustments down the road when you make some bigger changes to your swing.

OTHER EQUIPMENT CONSIDERATIONS

HE LAST TWO POINTS I'll make about fitting don't have anything to do with clubs. The kind of shoes you wear have a big impact on how you swing the club. If you wear very structured, classic shoes, you're going to have less foot action than if you wear something more like a sneaker. Some shoes feature higher heel platforms that can cause a great deal of restriction on ankle motion during the swing. This can lead to cramping and other swing issues. At the same time, if you are hypermobile in your ankles, you might need a more structured shoe. Regardless of the style you choose, be sure to walk around the store and simulate your swing to ensure you made the right choice. One last tip that goes for all your shoes. Once you find a style that works for your needs, be sure to buy a second pair. Happy feet go a long way in golf!

Finally, remember to buy gloves that properly fit your hands. Too often, I see golfers with gloves that are the wrong size and are littered with holes and wear patterns that compromise their ability to feel the club. To eliminate this problem, ask the professional staff at the course to help you get the right fit for your hands. It's also a good idea to have several in the bag always, so you keep a consistent feel when you grip the club. If you sweat a lot, be sure to rotate gloves throughout the round. You might even invest in some rain gloves for those hot summer days, or when you're playing in inclement weather. For those of you that play in colder climates, be sure to use hand warmers and gloves in between shots.

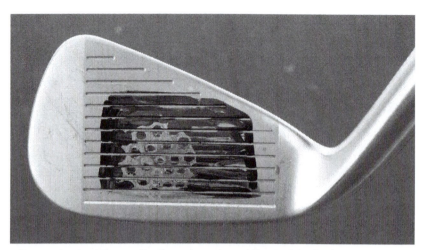

▷ One way to check the quality of your impact—and if your clubs fit—is to cover the face in dry erase marker. Don't worry. It wipes right off.

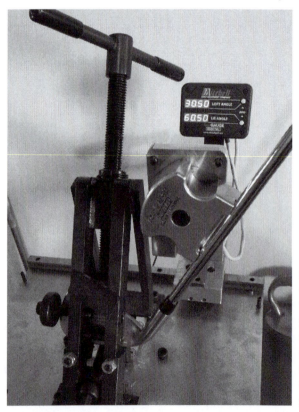

▷ A good clubfitter can use a lie/loft machine to tweak the specs on your irons in a matter of minutes. There's no excuse for playing a single hole with gear that doesn't fit your game.

CHAPTER 8

How to Enjoy The Game More

IN THIS CHAPTER

▷ Being a good partner is more than playing to your handicap

▷ How to be great host

▷ How to be a gracious guest

▷ New golfers, playing with your spouse, & junior golf

▷ What you can & can't learn from watching the tour

▷ Why your scores are consistently inconsistent

"In my 40 years in the game as a PGA Professional, I've come to find that people's enjoyment of the game has more to do with feeling welcome at the course and the people they are playing with, not the scores they shoot. When these ingredients are in play, golf is at it's best.

Don't fall into the trap of focusing on performance as being the indicator of your enjoyment of the game. Performance equals pressure. We all have enough of that in our life."

Dennis Satyshur

Director of Golf

Caves Valley Golf Club

1997 Ryder Cup Assistant Captain to Tom Kite

2009 PGA Bill Strausbaugh National Award Winner

ITTING BETTER SHOTS and shooting better scores are nice rewards, but they're really a means to an end. The goal is to enjoy yourself and enjoy the game. If you aren't having fun, you probably aren't going to continue to play over the long term.

That's why it's always been important to me to try to help my students have what I call a "complete" golf experience. That means getting the most out of the competitive and social components to the game.

One of the coolest things about golf is that the handicap system lets everybody play on a level playing field. If you're honest about keeping your score, your handicap will be a good predictor of what you will shoot during a regular round of golf.

Of course, some rounds aren't "regular!"

Competition is a big part of the game, and it comes in two flavors. You can play for yourself and try to win tournaments—at anything from the club level up to state amateur tournaments and even the pro game. And you can also play the classic two-person team game—like happens at member-guest tournaments and in leagues all over the country.

We've already talked a lot about the mental and physical skills you need to shoot great scores, and that advice is especially important for players who want to compete in individual tournaments.

Here, we're going to talk about the other part of competition—playing as a partner—and go over what you can do to enjoy that experience as much as possible. It's about learning the "relationship skills" that are going to help you both be a great partner on the course and have the full social experience that goes with playing as a part of a team.

What separates these from a lot of the other skills we've been talking about is that they're usually ones you have to pick up from experience— and from getting it wrong a few times. They're the subtle things nobody ever tells you—like the real way to pick a partner whose game and personality meshes with yours. Or, like what you should do when you're playing somebody who is obviously sandbagging—or playing to a handicap that isn't legitimate.

The way you respond to the good and not-so-good things that can come from partner golf is your "social handicap" and you're going to be judged by it at your club or among your playing buddies.

The second half of this chapter will be about helping you be a better fan. If you're sitting around the 19th hole talking about the latest tournament, or whether Tiger Woods was better than Jack Nicklaus, you want to come to those conversations with an informed opinion.

I'm not going to tell you what to think (even though my money would be on Jack). I'm just going to give you some tools to be able to look at tour player swings and understand what you're looking at. You'll learn the basics of comparing and contrasting them—and how to figure out what parts of the tour game are good for you to copy.

THE PARTNER GAME

F YOU SPEND ANY TIME around a decent size club—or you play in a regular league—you've probably noticed some trends. Some familiar names probably pop up as winners, either as a part of a regular pairing or matched with a variety of different players.

The players who consistently win team events do two things very well. They play to their handicap pretty consistently, and they bring out the best game in their partner.

Both pieces are extremely important to the puzzle. If you struggle to play to your handicap, you're obviously going to struggle to be competitive in team events. And if you're somebody who tends to, um, "outperform" your handicap consistently, you might get some short term support from partners who want to ride that train, but you're eventually going to bring unwanted attention to yourself.

When the handicap situation is fairly administered, you're going to be relatively evenly matched against most teams you play with. So what separates the players you can't wait to play with from the ones who never get more than one invitation?

Personality is a big piece of it. It doesn't mean you have to match up with somebody identical to you. But if you're playing in a member-guest, what you want is somebody who is going to give you a chance to be competitive—but also somebody you enjoy spending an extended period of time with.

There are players at every handicap level that enjoy playing when the shots count. I'm sure you know a guy who never breaks 90, but consistently plays to his full ability when it counts. He makes bogeys when he's supposed to make bogeys. That's just as valuable as somebody who is flirting with shooting par as 3-handicap.

The tougher pairing? A partner who might be a good player when he has time to spend on his game, but is coming in rusty. He might make a great birdie, but might also be in his pocket a lot. That pairing can work if it's with somebody very steady, but the unpredictability can be difficult to handle.

Another quality to avoid is the player who isn't invested in the day. If a few bad holes makes him or her pack it in and give up, or if he or she is on the phone a bunch in between shots, that's no fun. In the regular flights most players play in, there's plenty of ups and downs. We're talking about amateur golf. To get enraged by a bad shot or to give up after four or five holes just doesn't make sense—and makes for a long day.

You can go wrong at the opposite end of the spectrum too, with a partner that is so intense that it turns a match into a battle march. When that happens, it sometimes gets too hard to enjoy the day. You're always worried about your partner getting combative and saying the wrong thing to somebody.

Once you've made a good match personality-wise, it's nice to have a partner with a complementary game. For example, I think my strengths as a player are in wedge play, short game and putting. In a two-person event, I'd want to be paired with somebody who is a bomber and isn't afraid to take some risks.

It depends on the format, of course, but it you're a conservative straight hitter, you're going to be in most holes—which makes you the perfect candidate for a longer-hitting risk taker. Two bombers can also work well together, as long as both players can tolerate the roller-coaster of winning and losing a lot of holes. Being two down isn't a big problem if you're also making a lot of birdies to go with those holes when you're in your pocket. That's why it's always fun to watch what pairings go out in the Ryder Cup or the Solheim Cup, because it gives some insight into how the captains feel about playing styles and chemistry. Paul Azinger got a lot of attention for putting his players into pods of complementary skills and personalities. Hal Sutton obviously had a different opinion when he put Tiger Woods and Phil Mickelson together a few years before.

Whatever your playing style, you want to go play a round with somebody who is going to be your partner, and maybe even play a little money game with some random people you get paired with, so you can see how the team reacts to a little pressure. In the practice round, you can mess around with things like the hitting order off the tee and putting order on the green, to see how you both feel most comfortable. Sometimes a bomber wants to see a straight hitter get up there and hit one down the middle before he hits. Other times, he can't wait to go swing it and wants to go first. The practice round lets you work those things out ahead of time instead of trying to sort it out during a match.

Even in a team format, the goal is to stay as close to your regular game as you can. When you're counting every stroke, it isn't the time to start swinging wildly and trying shots you wouldn't otherwise try. Even if it works for a short time, when pressure builds later in the round or later in the event, you're going to be most comfortable doing what you usually do. If that means laying up on a par-4 or hitting an iron off the tee on a really narrow shot, you should do that.

HOW TO ENJOY THE DAY

ONE OF THE BIGGEST CHALLENGES for any guest that comes for a big tournament is handling the pressure of performing. If you hit a bunch of bad shots, it's natural to worry about being a disappointment, or wonder if you're going to get invited back. But I think I speak for most people when I say that the camaraderie and the experience are way more important than the scores you shoot. Everybody hits bad shots. It's a part of golf. It's how you handle those shots that determines how much you—and your partner—enjoy the day.

HOW TO BE A GREAT HOST

THE ADVICE IN THIS BOOK is designed to get you feeling better about your total experience in the game—from the time you flip on the television to when you drive up the driveway to the course, take a lesson or play a round. Your mindset obviously impacts all of those experiences.

If you play at the same course all of the time, it's easy to take this feeling for granted. You know everybody, and it feels good to check in with the pro, the bartender or the person who brings you a cart.

But no matter what kind of club or course you play regularly, you can always take a few easy steps to make the people you play with feel as good about the experience. For example, let's say you're going to bring a new person to play in a member-guest event at your place. Schedule a day long before the event and bring your friend for a visit. Introduce him or her to the pro and the other important people to the experience, and show your friend around the club. Just knowing where to park, where to go to change your shoes and who to ask if you have a question takes so much of the stress away from the private club experience.

This advice is equally true for the people in your family who might be new to the game. Golf can be intimidating, and there are plenty of unwritten rules to be worried about. If you want to introduce your spouse or child to the sport, you want it to be in an atmosphere that is fun and welcoming. If groups are breathing down your neck behind you and annoyed that you're spending a little more time showing your daughter or son how to hold the club, it's a bad look for everybody. There's nothing worse than playing with somebody and hearing them say afterward that they didn't enjoy it because they felt like an afterthought, or they were just "tolerated." That's a big piece of what we're trying to get rid of in this sport!

The professional staff at any course or club is going to want to help you with this situation. Go to your pro and ask when the best times are to go out when there won't be as many people on the course. Make the experience fun for the beginner, and it's going to be more enjoyable for you.

The same logic holds true when you have somebody you want to introduce to the world of instruction. If you have a spouse or a child interested in taking lessons, you want to be supportive and encouraging—not the person who turns a potential player off to the sport. If you're watching somebody you care about get a lesson, do just that—watch. Support what's happening in the lesson, even if you might disagree with it in the moment. The most important thing is to promote the connection with the instructor and let the teaching play out. If you intervene and question what's going on, you're just going to create tension. Wait until you're away from the practice area and have had a chance to have a full conversation with your spouse or child about the lesson before you make any conclusions about success, failure and what to do next.

Before offering your input, ask them if they had fun, and what they learned from the experience. Their perspective is most important and often not presented when their voice is not heard first. This is especially important after they play any round of golf, especially after a tournament round! If you ask most kids what takes the fun out of tournament golf, most will tell you "the car ride back from the tournament" because they dread hearing about what they did wrong from their parents. Do yourself a favor. Let them vent, show encouragement, avoid telling them what you think and share your feedback with their coach. This will save you a great deal of heartburn and time.

While we're on the subject of positives and negatives, this is a good time to talk about the best attitude you can carry with you when you're around people in the game. I've found that differences like handicap, money and "status" don't mean what people think they do when they're dealing with somebody who has an open, positive attitude.

If you're the person who is positive, polite and happy, and the one who would rather ask somebody about their game than give everybody on the tee a shot-by-shot rundown of your last round, you're going to do just fine. Resist the temptation to brag about your game, your club or where you've played around the world. One-uppers might get some short-term satisfaction about being the best or most worldly, but they don't get as many invitations to come back.

It works the same in the world of caddies. You can be the sour person who complains about getting the wrong yardage and blames the caddie for the bad swing you made. Or you can be the one who builds some rapport with the person who knows more about the course and the green contours and can be an asset. Play with positive karma and good things will come your way!

WATCHING THE GAME

WHEN YOU'RE HANGING AROUND the practice green with some friends or having a cocktail in the bar, what golf subject usually comes up first if you aren't talking about your own game?

It's almost always the tour—what players are doing, how far they're hitting it, what scores they're shooting. It's a fascinating subject, and there is no shortage of opinion—professional or otherwise.

I've always been interested in what tour players do, because I want to understand how they move and take any insight I can get from that and apply to my everyday work as an instructor. You might not be able to physically do what Dustin Johnson or Jason Day can do as athletes, but understanding what the "ideal" movements are for different body types can only help get us toward what it is ideal for you.

One of the best perks of being a member of the PGA of America is that the folks at Augusta National allow us to show our credentials and come in and watch The Masters every year. I'd be foolish if I didn't take advantage of that opportunity, and I've been going every year since 2005. I bring my video camera, and use it to record players during their early week practice. It's the ultimate stage to watch players prepare for one of the biggest tournaments of the year.

I watched Tiger Woods go through his complete practice routine that first year, in 2005, and he put on the coolest short game display I've ever seen. From the angle I was recording, you could see everything he was trying to do—from body motion to the approach of the club into the turf. He was in total control, and it was like taking a masters class in short game. Later that week he hit one of the most famous short game shots of all time, on the 16th green, and it was so interesting to see the prep work that led to the ability to hit that shot.

What Tiger's work really accentuated for me was that there was so much of the game—especially in short game—that teachers weren't giving to students. A tour player could get a lesson from a specialist, but the average player was still hearing that moving the ball back in his or her stance and hitting down on it with a 7-iron was a "safe" shot to go to around the green.

And that's what the tour is—the place where the players at the absolute top of the food chain are doing what they do. It's great to use those players as a model for what "ideal" is, and for informing a teaching curriculum, but there is some care you need to take when you look at what a player does and try to relate it to your own game.

I hear it all the time in those small talk conversations. Phil Mickelson makes this huge shoulder turn, so that means I should be doing that, too.

Then that player goes out and adds a new wrinkle to his swing—usually with scary bad results.

It really is one of the biggest risks I see when it comes to watching Tour golf on television, looking at swing sequences in the magazines or looking at all the slow-motion captures of swings you can see on YouTube. Everybody wants a magic potion that will cure their game in one swing—so they're susceptible to trying almost anything they read, hear or see.

But the golf swing really is a puzzle. Tour players have pieces that all fit together. Sometimes they make less-than-perfect motions, but make them in a way that meshes together in terrific compensations.

All you have to do is look at some of the greatest players of today—and great historical players—to see the amazing variety of ways players make solid contact. Fred Couples, Ben Hogan, Jason Day and Jim Furyk don't look anything alike. They don't swing anything alike. And the advice you'd give any of them about their swing would be very different than the advice you'd give somebody else.

Which means that it isn't as simple as watching Fred Couples hit balls and deciding to copy what he does with his elbow. You need to look at that swing as a whole, and consider what he's trying to do when he makes that swing. If you're determined to pattern what a tour player does in your own swing, make sure you pick a model that has a similar build type to you. If you're a short, stocky guy with a slashing swing, you're not going to do yourself any favors trying to copy Ernie Els. Go watch Ian Woosnam hit balls and absorb some of *that* flow instead.

I use the term "flow" on purpose, because it's a critical part of what makes a golf swing a *swing*. And it's why seeing players hit balls live, at a practice range, is so much different and more instructive than watching golf on television. When you see players live, you're getting a sense for their entire rhythm. You see how they work themselves into a shot. It's very methodical, very much on purpose, and incredibly consistent. They're not just going up and winging it. You could set it to music.

That *flow* is lost when you watch the game on television, and it's

really lost when you watch swings in slow motion during the analysis por-
tion of a telecast or on YouTube. Slow motion is great for examining the
details in a complex motion, but it can lead to players fixating on
static positions instead of the athletic motion in the swing. Seeing
Sergio Garcia with the club very flat at the beginning of his downswing
doesn't mean you should try to pose a flat position in your downswing.
His body and club are working together to get to that position during
a moment in time—but those pieces are on their way to somewhere
else. Rory McIlroy makes an incredibly rotary, fast swing, and he has
tremendous balance and support from the ground up—all the way
through the swing. If you aren't working on the entire sequence of
motion, you're missing out on what those great players are really doing,
and what they're doing might not be right for you! If you're a slicer,
trying to spin faster through the ball like Rory McIlroy will likely cause
you slice the ball even more if you haven't addressed your face to path
issues that are the likely culprit of your slice.

How do you find some of those matches? It starts with your predominant ball flight and how your trail arm works in the swing. Let's use Jack
Nicklaus as an example. He was an amazing ball-striker, and he pre-
ferred to hit a fade. In his prime, his swing was more upright than most,
and he had a "flying" right elbow" at the top. He hit the ball great because
his downswing began with a gliding motion to lower his arms and set up
his powerful release. If he had tried to start his downswing by turning
his hips hard like Ben Hogan advocated in *Five Lessons*, we would have
probably never heard of Jack Nicklaus.

TOUR EVENTS

F YOU ENJOY WATCHING those players play on television, you owe it
to yourself to go see an event live if you can. Walk around and see how
players handle competition and take in the drama, but don't miss out on
seeing the practice areas—both before the tournament on a Tuesday or

Wednesday and before and after the competitive rounds.

Watch how players prepare on the range—the clubs they hit and how long they spend with each one. Close your eyes and just listen to the sounds of pure contact. You won't find more of it anywhere else in the world than at a tour stop. During practice rounds, watch how players go through the process of scouting different holes. You'll instantly pick up some ideas about playing your own home course—like dropping balls around the green to figure out the easiest places to get up and down for certain hole locations. PGA Tour radio is also a great resource to add to your overall knowledge of the game. People like Hank Haney, Tony Ruggiero, Larry Rinker, Debbie Doniger and Ben Shear offer great perspective on your game and the tours every day.

FINAL PERSPECTIVE

WHETHER YOU'RE PLAYING in the U.S. Open or in a one-day event at your club, the difference between winning and losing isn't just who hits the best shots. It's who can recover best from the mistakes everybody invariably makes. If you know that over the green and left is dead on the hardest hole on your course, knowing where you have the easiest chip when you miss the green is going to make your target way, way bigger. That will give you some room to swing with less fear.

You don't have to swing anything like Rory or Sergio for that to help you.

Hitting better shots and shooting better scores are nice rewards, but they're really a means to an end. Although most golfers struggle with what I am about to tell you, it's vital you understand that inconsistency in scores is normal, at all levels of play. What does that mean? It means you only play to your handicap around 50% of the time. The good news is you'll outperform your handicap some of time but you'll play worse than your handicap just as much which is why you shouldn't beat yourself up when the scores don't match your Handicap.

To put this in perspective, take a look at the graph courtesy of Dr. Rick

Jensen from his book *"Easier Said Than Done"* which is a great read for any golfer to reinforce what it takes to improve your game.

As you look at the graph, you'll see the distribution of scores for Tiger Woods and Phil Mickelson from the 2000 season on the PGA Tour. When you look at Tiger's scoring range vs. Phil Mickelson's you can see why Tiger had such a dominant year on tour against Phil and the rest of the tour. You'll also see how Ron's (A 6-handicap golfer) scoring range appears on the bell curve and points to a scoring average of 82. If you ask most 6-handicaps what they think they should shoot, they will tell you mid to high 70's based a par of 72.

I'm all for shooting for the stars and setting goals that challenge my students to improve. Having said that, we all need to be wary of getting too caught up in expectations that are unrealistic relative to your current skill set which more often than not, is reflected by your stroke average. Focus on shooting scores that match or beat your stroke average and you'll have more fun on the course. Accept the volatility in your scores, enjoy the amazing journey golf offers you and your playing partners each time you play.

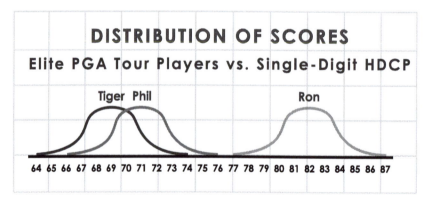

ACKNOWLEDGMENTS

▷ David Leadbetter, Bernie Najar and Jim Hardy
at the 2015 PGA Teaching Summit.

THE CONCEPT of *"The Game"* came about in May of 2015 with Tom Friedman and Matt Rudy. This project has gone through a number of revisions to provide the right content and I can't thank Matt and Tom enough for their help along the way. Additionally, Timothy Oliver has been a huge help with the graphics design and layout of the book. Lastly, getting this project to the finish line would not be possible without Alison Morrison who has worked tirelessly with me on the final edits and keeping me on track throughout the process.

There are not enough pages in this book for me to thank all those who deserve special recognition. I hope it is sufficient enough for me to say you know who you are and my gratitude is endless. However, my students are better off because of the following specific friends and mentors (in no particular order) who have been great sources of advice, technical expertise, and teaching insight:

ROD THOMPSON

My first exposure to golf was with Rod Thompson at Kenwood Country Club in Bethesda, Maryland at his junior camps in 1984. Rod is a consummate PGA Professional that made golf seem fun and exciting, which was exactly what sparked my interest in the game. To this day, we are close friends and share a common bond with the Plane Truth Certified Instructor Program, and out kicking our coverage with our wives.

KEN HEWITT AND GEORGE GALICH

During my childhood, I had the misfortune of losing my father, Andre Najar at a young age. Ken Hewitt sparked my interest in golf and I am forever grateful for his early guidance in golf and his contributions to our family. As I was graduating high school, George Galich came into our family as my step-father. His generosity, candid feedback, and entrepreneurial mindset was a breath of fresh air in our family. As I look back on this time in my life, these men were tremendous role models that helped me get through some tough times that I will never forget.

DAVID COHN & RICHARD KRESS

In 1987, I met David Cohn playing golf at Bethesda Country Club. At the time, he was one of the top commercial real estate brokers in the Washington Area who was always at the course. We became fast friends and played virtually every day in the afternoons until dark. At the time, David was taking regular lessons from David Leadbetter along with his best friend, Richard Kress. Both David and Richard have always been avid students of the game and have taken countless lessons from some of the top teachers in the game. I was fortunate they took a liking to me as a teenager and a new golfer. In 1988, they took me to see David Leadbetter for a lesson, which was a life changing experience. Since then, we have remained close friends and have shared many wonderful memories through golf.

DAVID LEADBETTER

Without question, the biggest reason so many golf professionals have the opportunity to make a great living teaching golf is because of David Leadbetter. I was extremely fortunate to meet David for couple lessons and to observe him teach at his golf school in my late teens. At the time, I had no idea how significant that time was in my life, but I'm forever grateful for that unique experience and his wisdom he has shared with all of us that teach the game.

WADE HEINTZELMAN

In 1988, I was walking in the streets of Bethesda and saw the Golf Care Center. In the store, there were hundreds of clubs including a refinishing area for persimmon and laminated woods for virtually all the clubs in the Washington area. At the time, Wade was also the golf coach at American University, and his prize pupil was his brother, Webb Heintzelman, who had just earned his PGA Tour Card. After a few visits to his shop to talk equipment, he asked if I would like to play sometime, which was an awesome experience and led to an amazing friendship. To this day, Wade and his partner, Jack Goldsby have been an tremendous resources for club fitting services with my players, and Wade is one of *Golf Digest's* Top-100 Fitters in the country. His enthusiasm and love of the game was a great role model for me on so many levels along with the coaching he gave me at American University. He's a terrific player in his own right, but an even better person who I am forever grateful to have met early in my golf career.

WAYNE DEFRANCESCO

One of the most important mentors in my career is Wayne DeFrancesco. In 1990, I met Wayne for a lesson that led to many more hours of watching him work with other players and discussing the golf swing. Additionally, I caddied for Wayne at several events including the 1991 Kemper Open and the PGA Tour Qualifying School. These were invaluable experiences along with teaching alongside him at Woodholme Country Club from 1996-2005. When it comes to playing and teaching golf, Wayne is a league of his own. In the world of internet lessons, he offers detailed analysis of tour player swings, online lessons, and much more at WayneDefrancesco.com.

JIM FOLKS, BILL STRAUSBAUGH, AND BOB DOLAN

Before my start in the golf business, I was extremely fortunate to sit down with Jim Folks, Bill Strausbaugh, and Bob Dolan. They each took the time out of their busy schedules to discuss the role of the PGA Professional in the golf business. At the time, like most twentysomethings, I had no clue how much went into becoming a successful PGA Professional and the responsibility we have for the game of golf. I am thankful that Jim, Bill and Bob were great role models and set me straight early on in my career.

ART AND LOLLIE SMITH

During my first year in the business, Art and Lollie took a special interest in me. They were members at the Suburban Club, where I got my first job. They encouraged me when I was just getting off the ground, and I'll always be grateful.

CHARLIE STAPLES

In May of 1994, I couldn't wait to get out the door to my first job in the golf business as an assistant professional at the Suburban Club in Baltimore, Maryland. Although it was just a seasonal job, I was thrilled for the opportunity and that's where my journey began, thanks to Mark Helffrich. As the golf season concluded, my plans were to head south, play some tournaments and find a place to teach golf during the winter months. At the time, I sent my resume to one of the most successful PGA Professionals of all time, Charlie Staples, who was the head of KSL Fairways and expressed interest in my services for one of his facilities. As it turned out, he had other plans for me, which turned into a full time teaching position, and I had the good fortune of spending lots of time watching Charlie in action and learned the importance of time management, setting goals, and how to run a successful business. Fast forward 20years, I was asked to speak at the 2015 PGA National Teaching and Coaching Summit on teaching with force plates and to bring a student for the live lesson. Charlie was all in and we had a great time on the biggest stage for a PGA Teaching Professional, which was amazing to share with Charlie, who has been an incredible mentor and father figure in my life. To this day, we still talk on a regular basis and he continues to guide me through my career.

MAC O'GRADY

In the fall of 1994, I attended Mac O'Grady's Instructor Symposium, which was a 3-day workshop that I will never forget. In attendance were some of the top instructors in the country, and seeing Mac in action was a tremendous learning experience. At the time, Mac and David Leadbetter were arguably the most sought out teachers in the game and it was really neat to hear Mac's perspective, see him strike the ball in person and to hear the most amazing sound of solid contact on his shots. To this day, I've only heard a handful of players with the same quality of strike, which he could achieve right-handed, left-handed, and even cross-handed! Along with his ball striking, I was so impressed with his passion and relentless pursuit to help his students during lessons.

MIKE BENDER

In January of 1995, after attending Mac O'Grady's Symposium, it was time to check in with one of Mac's early disciples, Mike Bender, for a follow-up lesson to build on what I learned from Mac at the seminar. At the time, Mike's Academy was at Timacaun Golf Club where he offered a comprehensive game improvement program to his students that featured a number of feedback stations to help students develop their skills. Seeing Mike's Academy — which by the way is one of the best in the country — was incredibly helpful and influential on how I've set up practice stations and training protocols with my students. Throughout my career, I've made multiple visits to his academy and always enjoy taking lessons from Mike on various aspects of the game. Mike has been a tremendous role model for me and so many instructors who have spent time learning from one of the brightest minds in golf.

LORIN ANDERSON

In 2007, I had the good fortune of being asked to join the AMF Teaching Division which is now the Proponent Group. At inception, many in the teaching industry were looking for specific resources that pertain to the business of teaching golf and unique educational and networking opportunities. Thanks to Lorin, I've been able to stay current with industry trends and learned so much from my peers in the group. In addition, he's been a tremendous resource and sounding board for career advice that has been invaluable to my career.

ED IBARGUEN

During my apprenticeship with the PGA, Ed was the facilitator for the Teaching Golf checkpoint where he gave us evaluations on our submitted lesson examples. His candid feedback and encouragement were extremely helpful. Throughout my career, he's always checked on my development and encouraged me along the way. In 2015, he asked me to present at the National PGA Teaching & Coaching Summit which was career milestone and an incredible honor. In addition, he encouraged me to become an adjunct teacher for the PGA to help out with the PGM Program, which has been a great experience on many levels. Ed is a tremendous role model for all PGA Professionals and I've been extremely fortunate to have met him early on in career.

MARTIN HALL

One of my best friends in the business is Martin Hall, who is one of the most passionate people you'll meet in the golf business and dedicated instructors in the game. As a lifelong student of the game, his wisdom and candid feedback has been invaluable to me throughout my career. I've had the good fortune to spend a great deal of time with Martin and his better half, #Pure (Lisa Hall) and they are an amazing duo. Despite being a launch monitor junkie who owns virtually every training aid and conceivable item from Home Depot to help golfers, he's been a tremendous mentor and an amazing friend throughout my career. Martin's contributions to the game are countless and his "School of Golf" Show on the Golf Channel has been a huge success because he is always coming up with new ways to help golfers improve their games. One of the biggest thrills of my career was presenting with Martin at the 2015 MAPGA Teaching Summit.

JIM HARDY

In 2007, I met Jim Hardy and attended one of his golf schools, which was quite an experience. At the time, he had recently released his best-selling book and video series, *"The Plane Truth For Golfers"* which was a hot topic of conversation in the teaching community. After spending several days watching Jim in action, it was clear to me that he was a fantastic communicator and had a gift for connecting with his students. When his instructor certification program became available, I enrolled in the program which has been a great way to improve my skills as an instructor and meet some amazing teachers in the program. Since then, Jim and I have become close friends and teach several golf schools together each year which is always a fun experience. Along with Jim, Chris O'Connell and Mike Crisanti have been great resources for me since becoming a Plane Truth Certified Instructor.

MIKE ADAMS

Mike has been a tremendous mentor to me and countless teaching professionals throughout his career. His depth of knowledge and relentless pursuit to help golfers and fellow teachers improve their skills is incredible. What I find most impressive about him is that he finds the good in all teaching philosophies and helps you understand how they will work with some players and why they won't work with others. Since getting to know Mike, we've spent countless hours discussing the many combinations that exist in the golf swing due to each golfer's unique physical characteristics, which he describes as "BioSwing Dynamics" with his partner, E.A. Tischler. Between the two of them, they have certified hundreds of teaching professionals across the country and throughout the world with this program. In addition, Mike has been working extensively with Swing Catalyst on how ground reaction forces relate to BioSwing Dynamics, and we are currently finishing an exciting book and video project with Dr. Scott Lynn, Ben Shear, and E.A. Tischler that will be available in the coming months.

MARK SWEENEY, AIMPOINT GOLF

In 2009, Mark Sweeney did an AimPoint demonstration at the Proponent Group Teaching Summit that caught my attention and was the start of my journey to become a better green reader through the AimPoint Certified Instructor Program. Over the past 9 years, it's amazing how much he has refined the system to make it user friendly for all level of golfers. Through the evolution of AimPoint, he has also added a number of resources for his certified instructors that are adding a new dimension to putting programs to help students shoot lower scores. Mark is truly a pioneer in golf with his revolutionary green reading system and has some really cool things in the pipeline to help golfers visualize the path of the putt. Since becoming the first AimPoint Certified Instructor in the Middle Atlantic Region, I've taught over a thousand students how to improve their green reading skills, improve their speed, aim, and course management thanks to Mark Sweeney.

KEVIN WEEKS

Through my travels at various teaching seminars, I became fast friends with Kevin Weeks, who is one of most passionate instructors in the business. Kevin has one of the best putting studios you'll see and loves doing research. On top of that, he's a wonderful coach and runs one the best junior programs in the country with his team at Cog Hill Golf Club. Spending time with Kevin is always entertaining and he's done a fantastic job presenting a number of my teaching seminars in the MAPGA on putting, short game, and junior programs. Despite being a Waffle House addict, he's great to spend time with and offers one of the best instruction programs in the country.

DR. RICK JENSEN AND HENRY BRUNTON

When it comes to helping teachers improve their coaching skills, Rick and Henry have done an excellent job with their coaching workshops. Since attending several of their programs, I've improved my coaching skills, knowledge of skill development, and the essential mental skills that can make or break performance on the course. Attending these workshops has been invaluable and I look forward to attending more in the future.

MICHAEL BENTLEY

One of the brightest minds in the golf industry is Michael Bentley. Throughout his career, he has helped develop some of the industry's most innovative products, including K-Vest, Enso, Blast 360, and the Leadbetter Putting System. Along with this, he's a tremendous coach and teaching professional to many of the game's top players on all major tours. Since meeting Michael early on in my career, I've learned a tremendous amount about 2D and 3D motion capture, joint alignment, golf specific exercise programs, and coaching strategies to help golfers improve all aspects of the game. His certification program has been a great resource for my continued professional development and countless other teaching professionals. Michael is a tremendous role model as teacher and coach, and a wonderful friend.

FITNESS & WELLNESS PROFESSIONALS

In 1996, I was working in South Florida as a private coach for Whit Staples. At that time, I had a unique opportunity to train with PETE DRAOVITCH who was Greg Norman's fitness trainer. Pete introduced me to the value of workouts for golfers and took me for my first 3D Motion Capture to assist with some research he was conducting with CHRIS WELCH, which was quite the experience in 1995! Another great resource I met early in my career was CHRIS VERNA a mobility specialist in South Florida who works with countless professional athletes and offers a unique program to his clients. At the time, I learned a bunch of mobility exercises from Chris that were extremely helpful for me and my students. From 1999-2003, I spent a great deal of time learning from DR. GREG ROSE and MIKE ROMATOWSKI who taught the "Advantage Golf" Certifications together. Following the program, I would train with Mike on a regular basis and was extremely fortunate to benefit from his knowledge of fitness training along with Charlie McMillin, who is an exceptional trainer and a resistance training specialist. For the next couple of years before Greg left Maryland to start TPI with DAVE PHILLIPS I spent as much time as I could learning from him whenever possible which helped me better understand the physical factors that influence how golfers swing the club. Since then, TPI has influenced countless golf, fitness, and medical professionals thanks to Greg, Dave, and their amazing team.

STACY DEVINE

Between 2008-2012 I was a train wreck, with injuries and chronic foot pain. After exhausting virtually all my options before having foot surgery, I met Stacy Devine in the summer of 2012. At my first session, which was to deal with a sciatic nerve back issue, she backed-tracked through the events that led up to my injuries and began to work her magic. Using a variety of techniques, along with helping me to understand how the body compensates for injury and protecting vital organs, was the key to my recovery. Since then, seeing her on a regular basis has been life changing and has helped me better understand the body and pain management. In addition, her perspective on motion restrictions has helped me better recognize patterns with students. Stacy is an angel to so many people and I'm forever thankful to find her during a difficult time in my life.

OZZIE NEWSOME AND JOHN HARBAUGH

In golf, you're always learning, especially from your students! Ozzie Newsome, has been a tremendous influence on how I teach and coach players. His candid feedback and the stories he has shared from his Hall of Fame Career are priceless. Special thanks to John Harbaugh and Ozzie Newsome for inviting me to watch practices with the Ravens. Watching these practices has been an invaluable experience. Along with that, these guys are wonderful friends that have taken a special interest in my career and my students that compete in tournaments. The wisdom and encouragement they share has been amazing and I'm a far better coach as a result.

JAMES LEITZ

One of the brightest minds in the golf business is my good friend, James Leitz. He's the only Top-100 Teacher and Club Fitter in the country and does a tremendous job educating fellow professionals. I've had the good fortune to learn a great deal from James with respect to Trackman, The D-Plane, and Gears Golf. His practical application to technology and commitment to excellence makes him a tremendous role model for fellow professionals.

DR. SCOTT LYNN, PHD

At the 2016 PGA Show, I had the good fortune to meet Dr. Scott Lynn, who is the Director of Research for Swing Catalyst and has a Ph.D. in BioMechanics. Through Swing Catalyst's continuing education and certification program, Scott is doing an amazing job educating all in attendance with practical applications for using this technology with students. After attending several workshops with Scott, we've become close friends and enjoy golf together when possible, and recently taught a Swing Catalyst Level 2 Certification in Germany and Sweden which was a great experience.

Writers and Magazines

TOM FRIEDMAN

One of the driving forces behind writing my first book is Caves Valley Member, Tom Friedman. I've had the pleasure of working with Tom on his game for several years and it's been great to see the progress he's made with his game. Spending time with him out on the course at Caves in a playing lesson is one of my favorite places to be. As a world traveler, he's always prepping for a unique golf experience during his lessons, which are often on the course. As a fierce competitor and someone that always has very specific performance goals, our sessions are intense, as you might expect. At the same time, there is plenty of conversation between shots where I've had the opportunity to ask him about his career, world affairs, and the process of writing books. It was so interesting to hear firsthand Tom's descriptions of how he put ideas to paper, and Tom has given me incredible encouragement to go out and write my own book. He's a wealth of information about so many topics, and he's become a wonderful friend.

MATT RUDY

Since getting to know Matt through my collaborations with *Golf Digest*, he was a natural fit to help me with my first book project. Throughout the process, Matt has been extremely helpful and candid with his feedback on how to write a successful golf book. During the process, he's been an invaluable sounding board and big help for staying on course to the finish line. Matt is a wonderful writer and extremely versed on the ever changing golf industry. His knowledge, wisdom, and friendship have made this project a fun experience that I will never forget.

GOLF DIGEST

Since 2000, I've had the good fortune to be recognized by my peers as a *Golf Digest* "Best Teachers in State." This has been a tremendous honor, along with being asked to contribute to a number of instruction articles and videos thanks to Matt Rudy and his team at *Golf Digest*. These experiences have been invaluable to my career and have been tremendous learning opportunities to improve my communication skills and organize my content for future projects.

DAVID DENUNZIO

Through my affiliation with *Golf Magazine*, I've had the opportunity to work with David DeNunzio on numerous instruction articles, videos, and as a presenter at *Golf Magazine's* 2014 Annual Top-100 Teachers Summit. Through these experiences, I've learned a great deal from that has helped me improve my communication skills and awareness of industry trends in the golf business. David is one of the funniest characters in the business and has done a great job of bringing teachers together to collaborate on various instruction pieces.

GOLF MAGAZINE

Since becoming a *Golf Magazine* Top-100 Instructor, I've had some unique opportunities to contribute to instruction articles and videos thanks to David DeNunzio and his team at *Golf Magazine*. This has been a huge boost to my career and I am forever grateful for the opportunities they have provided along the way.

PGA MAGAZINE AND GOLF RANGE MAGAZINE

At various points in my career, I've had the opportunity to contribute to *PGA Magazine* and *Golf Range Magazine* with best practices for teaching golf. Sharing ideas with fellow professionals is extremely rewarding and contributing to these platforms has been a tremendous honor.

Teaching Equipment/Technology/PXG

JC VIDEO SYSTEMS

Mark Connell and his team at JC Video has been huge help along the way with video and computer systems, and website design services.

K-MOTION

As one of the company's first customers, I've received wonderful customer support and education from Tony Morgan, Jason Meish, and Steve Diamond's amazing team at K-Motion. One of the best tools I've found to help students with body awareness is the K-Vest bio-feedback training mode. Being able to set specific programs for my students has improved the quality of their practice sessions and accelerated the learning process.

SWING CATALYST

One of the best investments I've made in teaching equipment is the Swing Catalyst Motion Plate and Video Software. This technology has been extremely helpful to better understand ground reaction forces and pressure mapping in golf swing. In addition, the software enables all the data from Trackman and video files to seamlessly integrate for easy reference and game tracking purposes. Along with great equipment, Swing Catalyst's continuing education programs with Dr. Scott Lynn have been extremely informative and helpful for expanding my knowledge of ground reaction forces.

MICHAEL NEFF & GEARS GOLF

3D motion technology continues to improve each year, and Gears Golf provides an incredible visual experience with their optical motion capture system. Whether you're doing a full body or club only capture, Gears Golf is an invaluable diagnostic tool thanks to Michael Neff and his team at Gear Golf. Since purchasing the system, I've learned so much from "Nipper" about club delivery considerations that influence release patterns that often result from lie angle issues you could never see without Gears 3D. In the fall of 2016, one of students, Kyle Berkshire, began training to compete on the World Long Drive Tour. When we did the initial assessment, Kyle would max his speed out at 127 mph and his driver would often reach a peak height of over 160 feet! While it was obvious it was flying too high, the real culprit was dialing the correct shaft, loft, and club length combination. It was also critical to find opportunities to increase his swing efficiency which was very much like looking for a needle in the haystack. Fortunately, we found some opportunities by looking under the hood with Gears and Kyle picked up 20 mph of club speed over the next 6 months and now uses a Driver that has 2.5 Degrees of loft as compared to his original 8.5 Degree Driver. Fast forward to September 2017, Kyle reached the semi-finals at the 2017 World Long Drive Championships as a rookie and is excited for another shot at the title in 2018.

PXG

Throughout my career, I've had the opportunity to work with the majority of OEMs and fit countless golfers for equipment. Since joining PXG's National Staff in 2015, I've had tremendous support from their team of engineers and access to the best equipment available which has been a great addition to my club fitting services. PXG's founder, Bob Parsons is a true innovator that has had an amazing impact on the golf industry, which is making the other OEMs step up their game for quality and performance. Being a part of the PXG Team has been a breath of fresh air and I'm thrilled to be a part of their team!

Finally, a special thanks to my students, who teach me every day.

Printed in Great Britain
by Amazon